STUDENT INSTRUCTION MANUAL

INTENSIVE RECORDS MANAGEMENT

FIFTH EDITION

Andrea Henne, Ed.D.

Dean
Online Education and Distributed Learning
San Diego Community College District

SOUTH-WESTERN
CENGAGE Learning

Australia • Brazil • Japan • Korea • Mexico • Singapore • Spain • United Kingdom • United States

Intensive Records Management, 5E
Andrea Henne, Ed.D.

VP/Editorial Director
Jack W. Calhoun

VP/Editor-in-Chief
Karen Schmohe

Acquisitions Editor
Jane Phelan

Project Manager
Dr. Inell Bolls

Consulting Editor
Marianne Miller

Marketing Manager
Valerie A. Lauer

Ancillary Coordinator
Kelly Resch

Manufacturing Coordinator
Charlene Taylor

Marketing Coordinator
Kelley Gilreath

Production House
Interactive Composition Corporation

Printer
Graphics Management

Art Director
Linda Helcher

CONTENTS

PREFACE

The records management field is undergoing many changes due to technological transformations and new laws and regulations. *Intensive Records Management*, Fifth Edition, provides current information and best practices in the field, reflecting those changes. *Intensive Records Management*, Fifth Edition, introduces basic concepts that form the foundation of how to manage records. You will have the opportunity to reinforce your learning of records management concepts with Practical Applications. The author, Dr. Andrea Henne, has created a simulation that provides hands-on practice in applying those concepts. Dr. Henne is an experienced educator, business consultant, instructional technologist, and author with extensive background in business information management systems.

The major objective of this simulation is to provide the records management rules, practices, and applications you will need for future employment in entry-level information management careers. Upon successful completion of the simulation, you will be able to:

- **manage records through their entire life cycle by using rules compatible with ARMA International, the leading authority in records management.**
- **use alphabetic, consecutive numeric, terminal-digit numeric, subject, and geographic filing procedures.**
- **explain the benefits of color-coding files.**
- **apply the processes of records retention, transfer, and disposition.**
- **define databases and create tables to add, modify, sort, search, and print records.**
- **use records management vocabulary.**

To simulate through actual practice, *Intensive Records Management*, Fifth Edition, uses a variety of documents that flow in and out of an organization. The simulation is organized to allow you to progress at your own rate; specific directions are given for each task. Electronic filing exercises can be completed using any popular commercial database software available in the classroom. You simply input data from the instruction book into the database program and complete the activities as instructed.

The simulation includes the following materials:

- *Student Instruction Manual*
- **Data CD**
- **Checksheet Packet**
- **Forms Pad 1**
- **Forms Pad 2**
- **Forms Pad 3**
- **Forms Pad 4**
- **Files Box**
- **Envelope 1 (with 11 guides and pressure-sensitive labels)**
- **Envelope 2 (with 9 folders)**
- **Envelope 3 (with 10 folders)**

ALPHABETIC INDEXING RULES

Rule 1: Indexing Order of Units
A. **Personal Names.** (1) The surname is the key unit. (2) The first name or initial is the second unit. (3) The middle name or initial is the third unit.
B. **Business Names.** Index in the order written on the letterhead or trademark.

Rule 2: Minor Words and Symbols in Business Names
(1) Articles, prepositions, conjunctions, and symbols are separate indexing units. (2) Symbols are spelled in full. (3) When *The* appears as the first word of a business name, it is the last indexing unit.

Rule 3: Punctuation and Possessives
Disregard all punctuation when indexing personal and business names.

Rule 4: Single Letters and Abbreviations
A. **Personal Names.** (1) Initials in personal names are separate units. (2) Abbreviated personal names are separate units and are not spelled out.
B. **Business Names.** (1) Single letters are indexed as written. (2) Each letter is a separate unit when a space separates the letters. (3) Letters written without spaces are one unit. (4) Abbreviated words and names are one unit. (5) Acronyms, which are names made up of initial letters of words, are one unit. (6) Radio and television station call letters are one unit.

Rule 5: Titles and Suffixes
A. **Personal Names.** (1) All titles used with full personal names are the last unit. (2) Professional or seniority suffixes are the last unit. (3) Numeric suffixes come before alphabetic suffixes. (4) The title is the last unit when a name contains both a suffix and a title. (5) A title followed by a first name or a surname only is indexed as written.
B. **Business Names.** All titles are indexed as written.

Rule 6: Prefixes—Articles and Particles
An article or a particle is combined with the part of the personal or business name following it to form one indexing unit. Spaces and punctuation are disregarded.

Rule 7: Numbers in Business Names
(1) Arrange spelled-out numbers alphabetically. (2) Arrange numbers in digit form in ascending order before all alphabetic letters or words. (3) Arrange Arabic numerals before Roman numerals. (4) Arrange inclusive numbers by the first digits. (5) Ignore *st, d,* and *th.*

Rule 8: **Organizations and Institutions**

Index organizations and institutions as written on the letterhead. When *The* appears as the first word in an organization or institution name, it is the last unit.

Rule 9: **Identical Names**

Filing order of identical names is determined by the addresses. Compare addresses in this order: (1) city names, (2) state or province names, (3) street names, (4) house or building numbers.

Rule 10: **Government Names**

Index all government names first by the name of the government unit—country, state, county, or city. Next, index the distinctive name of the department, agency, bureau, office, board, and so on. Index the distinctive translated English name of a foreign government name as the first unit followed by the rest of the name.

TWO-LETTER POSTAL ABBREVIATIONS UNITED STATES, DISTRICT, POSSESSION, OR TERRITORY

AL	Alabama		MT	Montana
AK	Alaska		NE	Nebraska
AZ	Arizona		NV	Nevada
AR	Arkansas		NH	New Hampshire
CA	California		NJ	New Jersey
CO	Colorado		NM	New Mexico
CT	Connecticut		NY	New York
DE	Delaware		NC	North Carolina
DC	District of Columbia		ND	North Dakota
FL	Florida		OH	Ohio
GA	Georgia		OK	Oklahoma
GU	Guam		OR	Oregon
HI	Hawaii		PA	Pennsylvania
ID	Idaho		PR	Puerto Rico
IL	Illinois		RI	Rhode Island
IN	Indiana		SC	South Carolina
IA	Iowa		SD	South Dakota
KS	Kansas		TN	Tennessee
KY	Kentucky		TX	Texas
LA	Louisiana		UT	Utah
ME	Maine		VT	Vermont
MD	Maryland		VI	Virgin Islands
MA	Massachusetts		VA	Virginia
MI	Michigan		WA	Washington
MN	Minnesota		WV	West Virginia
MS	Mississippi		WI	Wisconsin
MO	Missouri		WY	Wyoming

Chapter 1: Basic Records Management Concepts

Learning Goals

- Become familiar with the contents and organization of *Intensive Records Management,* Fifth Edition.
- Learn the importance of records management in an organization.
- Learn the records management terms used throughout the text.
- Learn the first two steps in the cycle of records management: creating records and using records.

Introduction

Every day in offices, schools, business organizations, and government agencies, records are created, sent, received, stored, searched for, and sometimes even misplaced. Maintaining a systematic approach to the ever-increasing flow of records and the information they contain is quite a challenge! By becoming proficient in records management, you and your skills will be an asset to any organization.

Intensive Records Management, Fifth Edition, prepares you to work with a variety of office records by giving you hands-on practice with five methods of filing: alphabetic, consecutive numeric, terminal-digit numeric, subject, and geographic. Based on the most recent professionally recognized filing guidelines, these methods are the foundation for understanding electronic filing and using computer databases.

Each of the five methods of filing is presented with examples and illustrations. Use the Check Your Understanding exercises to help determine whether you need to review the material or whether you are ready to complete the filing projects, called Practical Applications.

The 10 Practical Applications provide you with the opportunity to apply the rules and procedures of records management. In addition to the Practical Applications, which require you to follow the steps for storing records, you will complete six Retrieval Exercises. Those exercises measure your ability to find the records you have filed. Each Retrieval Exercise is timed to reflect the need for efficient, accurate retrieval of records in business offices.

Beginning with Practical Application 2B, you will see Computer Applications. Complete the computer activities as instructed in Appendix A, "Computer Applications."

COMPUTER APPLICATION

Why Is Records Management Important?

Information is one of the most important resources of an organization. Records management is important because it creates a systematic way to make needed documents and information easily accessible. Without an efficient way to organize the vast amount of information that flows through an organization, the following results are common:

- **Valuable documents may be misplaced.**
- **Time and productivity are lost in the search for missing information.**
- **Resources are wasted on maintaining expensive storage facilities.**

Today's organizations are required to comply with legal and legislative requirements for ensuring the privacy and security of records. Certain records must be easily accessible for audits and for providing evidence of past actions and decisions. Organizations rely on a system of records management for handling disaster recovery, for backing up critical records, and for safekeeping of corporate knowledge.

The Cycle of Records Management

Records (and the information they contain) have a life cycle. As illustrated in Figure 1-1, the life cycle of a record begins with **creation** and ends with **disposition.** In Chapters 2–6, you will learn how to work with records in their storage and retrieval phases; in Chapter 7, you will learn how to manage records when their active life has ended.

Creation of Records

A record may be created by using forms; word processing, spreadsheet, database, or other computer software; or e-mail. Records may be received through the postal service, a delivery service or courier, fax, web sites, e-mail, interoffice mail, or customer contact. A record may be in the form of paper, discs, digital files, or microimage media. Drawings, photographs, and reports are also types of records. The creation phase is the beginning of the cycle of records management.

CREATION ▸ USE ▸ STORAGE ▸ RETRIEVAL ▸ DISPOSITION

FIGURE 1-1
Complete Cycle of Records Management

Use of Records

The second phase in the life cycle of a record is its **use.** The information contained in records has value for making decisions, conducting research, and gaining knowledge. In a computerized records system, a person can readily use information contained in a group of related records, called a **database.** Guidelines for access and use of records need to be established within an organization to ensure the security and privacy of records.

Impact of Technology on Records Management

Recent dramatic corporate scandals have brought records management (or the lack of records management) into the spotlight. The rapid increase in the number of electronic documents—particularly e-mails, but also image files, audio files, and video files—has presented a challenge for records managers. Organizations are vulnerable to lawsuits when required documentation and records are not readily accessible or when vital records have been destroyed.

Electronic document creation and management have changed the way organizations handle information. Technology can reduce the costs of paper storage, make it easy to share documents with multiple offices and with clients, reduce the amount of time needed to retrieve documents, improve security and disaster preparedness, and meet compliance and legal requirements more efficiently. By implementing computerized systems, people in an organization are able to:

- **store records in searchable databases.**
- **automatically manage schedules for retaining and destroying records.**
- **track access to electronic and paper-based records.**
- **track the location of records in boxes, tapes, and other external storage media.**

To help manage the proliferation of electronic documents, records management software is becoming a necessity. However, whatever records management software is used, the system needs to be based on an organization's policies and procedures for appropriate creation, use, retention, and destruction of records.

Records Management Vocabulary

Study this list of vocabulary words to become familiar with the records management terms used throughout *Intensive Records Management,* Fifth Edition.

Accession log—A list of the code numbers assigned to each record that shows the next available code number in a numeric filing system; also called an **accession book** or a **number list.** See the illustration in Chapter 4 on page 56.

Bar code—A unique pattern of printed vertical lines and spaces containing information that is read electronically.

BEST PRACTICES

Keeping Up with Changes in Records Management

How can a busy professional learn about the latest developments in the field of records management? One of the best ways is to take advantage of the wealth of resources provided by ARMA International, the leading authority in the field of records management. With more than 10,000 members, ARMA International, a nonprofit organization, represents professionals who work as records managers, archivists, librarians, imaging specialists, legal professionals, IT managers, consultants, and educators. ARMA members come from a wide range of organizations in the United States, Canada, and more than 30 other countries around the world.[1]

On the ARMA International web site at http://www.arma.org, you have access to

- legislative and regulatory updates.
- standards and best practices.
- technology trends and applications.
- live and web-based education.
- marketplace news and analysis.
- books and videos on managing records and information.

ARMA publishes *The Information Management Journal* bimonthly. The *IMJ* is a great source of information. It contains articles written by experts in the field and the latest news and developments. The ARMA web site has a convenient search option that you can use to locate articles on specific topics of interest and order a copy of the article from the online ARMA bookstore. Keeping up with changes in records management is much easier, thanks to ARMA International.

[1] *Source: ARMA International, 30 July, 2005 http://www.arma.org/about/overview/index.cfm.*

CD-R (compact disc–recordable)—An optical disc to which data can be recorded once and read many times. See also **WORM**.

CD-ROM (compact disc read-only memory)—An optical disc containing prerecorded information that cannot be modified or erased.

CD-RW (compact disc–rewritable)—An optical disc on which data can be recorded and rewritten.

Charge-out and follow-up—The procedure for fulfilling requests to borrow records and for making sure that records are returned on time and refiled correctly.

Coding—Marking the units in the name or subject under which a record will be filed.

Correspondence—Incoming and outgoing communication in written form.

Cross-reference—An entry directing attention to one or more related headings. A cross-reference directs a person to look elsewhere for a record or for more information.

Database—A file of related records, all of which share the same fields; for example, a customer database could contain 150 records (or customers), each of which has fields for name, address, and telephone number.

Digital record—Created by a computer system.

DVD (digital versatile disc)—An optical disc with a variety of formats, including **DVD-ROM** (prerecorded/read-only) and **DVD-R/RW** (recordable once/rewritable).

E-mail (electronic mail)—Incoming and outgoing messages received and sent electronically by way of computer networks.

Fax (facsimile)—A machine that scans a document and converts it to electronic signals. The receiving fax machine converts the signals and prints out a copy of the document, called a fax or facsimile.

Field—In an electronic record or form, a position (column) set aside for a specific type of information. Each item of information in a computer file; for example, in a customer file, there are fields for name, street address, city, state, ZIP Code, and telephone number.

File—A collection of related records arranged in a systematic way and stored either manually or electronically.

Filing—Arranging records into predetermined sequences, such as alphabetic, numeric, subject, or geographic.

Filing indexing unit—A number, letter, or word or any combination of these used as part of the filing segment.

Filing segment—The entire name, subject, or number used for filing purposes.

CHECK YOUR UNDERSTANDING

Basic Records Management Concepts   Time Goal: 5 Minutes

Directions: Match each records management definition on the left with its vocabulary term on the right. Write the letter of your answer in the space provided.

Answer	Definition
_____	1. One of the most important resources in an organization.
_____	2. Incoming and outgoing communication in written form.
_____	3. A symbol placed on a record, indicating that the record is ready to be filed.
_____	4. All materials preserved for future reference.
_____	5. A collection of related records arranged in a systematic way.
_____	6. A comprehensive list of types of records that indicates for each type how long it is to be maintained and when it may be transferred or destroyed.
_____	7. A file of related records, all of which share the same fields.
_____	8. Records photographed in reduced sizes and stored on microfilm or microfiche.
_____	9. An entry in a file that directs a person to look elsewhere for a record or for more information.
_____	10. Marking the units in the name or subject under which a record will be filed.

Vocabulary Term
A. Database
B. Information
C. Release mark
D. Correspondence
E. Microimage records
F. Records retention and disposition schedule
G. Records
H. Cross-reference
I. File
J. Coding

See page 127 for the correct answers to this Check Your Understanding exercise.

WORKPLACE FOCUS

Would You Like a Career in Records Management?

Records managers manage the corporate memory of an organization by managing the information created and received by organizations. This includes digital information such as e-mail and electronic documents as well as paper-based letters and reports.

Alternative Titles

- **Knowledge Manager**
- **Records Supervisor**
- **Records Coordinator**
- **Information Services Administrator**

Tasks and Duties

Records managers may do all or some of the following:

- **Manage the records of an organization**
- **Use records management systems to track the movement of records**
- **Devise and maintain classification systems to store records so they can be easily retrieved.**
- **Control access to information**
- **Advise on records management policies and procedures**
- **Determine which records can be disposed of and oversee their disposal**
- **Oversee information technology changes relevant to records management**
- **Ensure that records management systems meet administrative, legal, regulatory, and financial requirements**
- **Oversee transfer of information from paper to digital**
- **Provide training on records management systems**

Skills

Records managers need to have project management, communication, and computer software skills. Useful skills include experience in using electronic databases and managing projects and staff members.

Knowledge

Records managers need to understand records management principles and guidelines as well as the different filing methods as they apply to paper-based and electronic systems.

Personal Qualities

Records managers need to maintain confidentiality when dealing with sensitive documents, demonstrate good judgment, and use interpersonal skills.

Physical Requirements

Records managers may be required to have a reasonable level of fitness as they may be required to carry heavy files and be on their feet for long periods.

Entry Requirements

Records managers may be required to undergo security checks if they are dealing with sensitive information

Source: Career Services, Kiwi Careers
(http://www.kiwicareers.govt.nz).

Guide—A divider with a captioned tab that is used to separate and identify sections in a file to facilitate retrieval of records.

Indexing—Selecting the filing segment under which to store a record and determining the order in which the units should be considered.

Information—Data that are contained in records and that are useful or meaningful.

Microimage records—Records are photographed in reduced sizes and stored on microfilm or microfiche.

OCR (optical character recognition)—The process of scanning printed characters or photos and converting them to digital format.

Records—All materials preserved for future reference (correspondence, documentary materials, forms, books, microimage media, discs, machine-readable materials, photographs, computer printouts, and so on).

Records manager—The person responsible for controlling the creation, use, storage, retrieval, disposition, maintenance, protection, and preservation of an organization's records.

Records retention and disposition schedule—A list of types of records that indicates for each type how long it is to be maintained and when it may be destroyed.

Release mark—A symbol placed on a record, usually in the form of initials, a code, or a stamp, indicating that the record is ready to be filed.

WORM (write once, read many)—An optical disc that allows data to be written or recorded once and read many times.

End-of-Chapter Activity

Learn about professional records managers by visiting the ARMA International web site at http://www.arma.org. Click the link **About Us.** Read through the information; then browse through the **Job Search** section. In the following space, write a paragraph that describes the types of career development opportunities made available through the ARMA web site.

Chapter 2: Alphabetic Indexing Rules

> **Learning Goals**
> - Learn the rules for indexing personal and business names.
> - Index, code, cross-reference, sort, and file names on cards.
> - Retrieve cards from your card file within a specified time limit.

Introduction

Every organization relies on a systematic approach for managing the flow of records. The foundation of every effective records management system is a standardized set of rules and procedures that everyone in an organization follows. In this chapter, you will begin your hands-on application of the indexing rules and the procedures for basic records processing.

Indexing refers to selecting the filing segment under which a record will be filed. By following a standardized set of rules, records managers within a company have a consistent way of storing and retrieving records. ARMA International, the professional organization for the records management field, recommends the following seven Simplified Filing Standard Rules for consistency in filing.[1]

1. **Alphabetize by arranging files in unit-by-unit order and letter-by-letter within each unit.**

2. **Each filing unit in a filing segment is to be considered. This includes prepositions, conjunctions, and articles. The only exception is when the word *the* is the first filing unit in a filing segment. In that case, *the* is the last filing unit. Spell out all symbols—for example, &, $, #—and file alphabetically.**

3. **File "nothing before something." File single-unit filing segments before multiple-unit filing segments.**

4. **Ignore all punctuation when alphabetizing. This includes periods, commas, dashes, hyphens, apostrophes, and so on. Hyphenated words are considered one unit.**

5. **Arabic and Roman numerals are filed sequentially in ascending order (from lowest to highest) before alphabetic characters. All Arabic numerals precede all Roman numerals.**

---

[1] ARMA International, *Establishing Alphabetic, Numeric, and Subject Filing Systems*, 2005.

6. Acronyms, abbreviations, and radio and television station call letters are filed as one unit.

7. File under the most commonly used name or title. Cross-reference under other names or titles that might be used in an information request.

The 10 alphabetic indexing rules that follow provide more detailed directions for filing personal, business, and government names.

Rules for Indexing Personal and Business Names

The 10 indexing rules and examples in this chapter are consistent with ARMA's simplified rules. Each Check Your Understanding exercise is designed to evaluate your ability to apply the indexing rules. If you have difficulty completing any of the exercises, review the appropriate rules before continuing.

Alphabetize the names by comparing the letters in each unit until you find a difference. Compare the second units when the first units are the same. When the first and second units are the same, compare the third units, and so on.

Rule 1: Indexing Order of Units

A. Personal Names. A personal name is indexed this way: (1) the surname (last name) is the key unit, (2) the given name (first name) or initial is the second unit, and (3) the middle name or initial is the third unit. If determining

	Indexing Order of Units[2]		
Name	Key Unit	Unit 2	Unit 3
1. B. Ramon	RAMON	B	
2. Berta Ramon	RAMON	BERTA	
3. Debra Ramos	RAMOS	DEBRA	
4. Denise Ramos	RAMOS	DENISE	
5. Eduardo Ramos	RAMOS	EDUARDO	
6. Victor Ramosa	RAMOSA	VICTOR	
7. Victor Ramoso	RAMOSO	VICTOR	
8. Rachna Singh	SINGH	RACHNA	
9. Rachna R. Singh	SINGH	RACHNA	R
10. Rachna S. Singh	SINGH	RACHNA	S
11. Edward Song	SONG	EDWARD	
12. Danh T. Tran	TRAN	DANH	T
13. E. A. Tran	TRAN	E	A

EXAMPLES: RULE 1A

[2] The units in the Indexing Order of Units sections are shown in capital letters with no punctuation to correspond to the format used on folder label captions and file cards. The underlined letters show how the alphabetic order is determined.

the surname is difficult, consider the last name as the surname and cross-reference the name. (See the "Preparing Cross-Reference Cards" section on pages 16–18 for further explanation.)

Initials are considered separate indexing units. A unit consisting of just an initial precedes a unit that consists of a complete name beginning with the same letter. Remember, *nothing goes before something*. Punctuation is omitted.

B. Business Names. Business names are indexed as written, using company letterheads (or any registered business name) or trademarks as guides. Each word in a business name is a separate unit. Compound business or place names with spaces between the parts of the name are considered separate units. (For example, both *Ultra Star Theater* and *Up Town Footwear* have three units.)

Business names containing personal names are indexed in the order written, as are names of newspapers and magazines. For newspapers having identical names, use the city name as the last indexing unit.

EXAMPLES: RULE 1B

Name	Indexing Order of Units			
	Key Unit	Unit 2	Unit 3	Unit 4
1. Hillman Dry Cleaners	HILLMAN	DRY	CLEANERS	
2. J. Hillman Photo Studio	J	HILLMAN	PHOTO	STUDIO
3. J. J. Hillman Flowers	J	J	HILLMAN	FLOWERS
4. Jessica Lee Hair Salon	JESSICA	LEE	HAIR	SALON
5. Jewelry International	JEWELRY	INTERNATIONAL		
6. London Times Magazine	LONDON	TIMES	MAGAZINE	
7. Lubbock Daily News	LUBBOCK	DAILY	NEWS	
8. Neil Lubbock Electronics	NEIL	LUBBOCK	ELECTRONICS	
9. News Journal (Atlanta)	NEWS	JOURNAL	ATLANTA	
10. News Journal (Austin)	NEWS	JOURNAL	AUSTIN	
11. South West Designs	SOUTH	WEST	DESIGNS	
12. Southwest Airlines	SOUTHWEST	AIRLINES		

Rule 2: Minor Words and Symbols in Business Names

Articles, prepositions, conjunctions, and symbols are considered separate indexing units. Symbols are considered as spelled in full. When the word *The* appears as the first word of a business name, it is the last indexing unit. The following articles, prepositions, conjunctions, and symbols are frequently used in business names:

Articles:	*a, an, the*
Prepositions:	*at, by, for, in, of, off, on, out, over, to, with*
Conjunctions:	*and, but, or, nor*
Symbols:	*&, ¢, #, $, % (and, cent or cents, number or pound, dollar or dollars, percent)*

EXAMPLES: RULE 2

Name	Indexing Order of Units			
	Key Unit	Unit 2	Unit 3	Unit 4
1. Candy & Cards Center	CANDY	AND	CARDS	CENTER
2. ¢ Off Grocery Store	CENTS	OFF	GROCERY	STORE
3. The Computer Shop	COMPUTER	SHOP	THE	
4. Discount $ Shoe Outlet	DISCOUNT	DOLLAR	SHOE	OUTLET
5. For Your Health Drugstore	FOR	YOUR	HEALTH	DRUGSTORE
6. Forever Young Spa	FOREVER	YOUNG	SPA	
7. In Touch Massage	IN	TOUCH	MASSAGE	
8. # Time Watch Repair	NUMBER	TIME	WATCH	REPAIR
9. Over the Rainbow Tours	OVER	THE	RAINBOW	TOURS
10. Overland and Sons	OVERLAND	AND	SONS	
11. Up & Down Contractors	UP	AND	DOWN	CONTRACTORS
12. Uptown On Main Street	UPTOWN	ON	MAIN	STREET

CHECK YOUR UNDERSTANDING

Rules 1 and 2   Time Goal: 10 Minutes

Directions: Write the following 10 personal and business names in indexing order. Use capital letters and omit punctuation. Write the first units under Key Unit, the second units under Unit 2, and so on. Then alphabetize the names by numbering them from 1 to 10. Place the numbers in the parentheses provided.

Name	Indexing Order of Units			
	Key Unit	Unit 2	Unit 3	Unit 4
( ) L. Carmen Quinares				
( ) Lydia Quinares				
( ) L. C. Quinares				
( ) Quinn Fine Flooring				
( ) Quinares & Benes Investments				
( ) L. Carmen Quinaro				
( ) # Off Weight Loss				
( ) Off & On Electricians				
( ) Sunday News (Tucson)				
( ) Sunday News (Tyler)				

See page 127 for the correct answers.

Rule 3: Punctuation and Possessives

All punctuation is disregarded when indexing personal and business names. Apostrophes, commas, dashes, exclamation points, hyphens, periods, question marks, quotation marks, and diagonals (/) are disregarded, and names are indexed as written.

EXAMPLES: RULE 3

	Indexing Order of Units			
Name	Key Unit	Unit 2	Unit 3	Unit 4
1. Monica Raleigh-Lee	RALEIGHLEE	MONICA		
2. Sue-Ellen Ranji	RANJI	SUEELLEN		
3. Tarun R. Ranji	RANJI	TARUN	R	
4. Self-Serve Market	SELFSERVE	MARKET		
5. South-West Interior Designs	SOUTHWEST	INTERIOR	DESIGNS	
6. Uncle Sam's Health/Diet Foods	UNCLE	SAMS	HEALTHDIET	FOODS
7. United "A-One" Air Lines	UNITED	AONE	AIR	LINES
8. Univeras' Furniture	UNIVERAS	FURNITURE		
9. Univera's Real Estate	UNIVERAS	REAL	ESTATE	
10. Vend-O-Matic Equipment	VENDOMATIC	EQUIPMENT		
11. What's Up? Investigators	WHATS	UP	INVESTIGATORS	

Rule 4: Single Letters and Abbreviations

A. Personal Names. Initials in personal names are considered separate indexing units. Abbreviated personal names (for example, Chas., Jos., Theo., Thos., Wm.) and nicknames (for example, Ally, Barb, Chuck, Joe), are indexed as written. Disregard punctuation.

EXAMPLES: RULE 4A

	Indexing Order of Units			
Name	Key Unit	Unit 2	Unit 3	Unit 4
1. W. Dougherty	DOUGHERTY	W		
2. W. J. Dougherty	DOUGHERTY	W	J	
3. Will Dougherty	DOUGHERTY	WILL		
4. Wm. Dougherty	DOUGHERTY	WM		
5. Jos. Douglas	DOUGLAS	JOS		
6. Thos. Douglass	DOUGLASS	THOS		
7. Tom Douglass	DOUGLASS	TOM		
8. Chas. Douzjian	DOUZJIAN	CHAS		
9. Joe Dowell	DOWELL	JOE		
10. Edw. Dowler	DOWLER	EDW		

WORKPLACE FOCUS

The High Cost of Managing Paper

One of the factors driving the change from paper to electronic records is the high cost of managing paper. Research conducted by analyst firms such as the Gartner Group and Forrester report that:

- **1 in 10 documents will be misfiled and permanently lost.**
- **it costs, on average, $150 to find a missing document.**
- **it costs up to $350 to re-create a lost document.**
- **many workers spend an average of one hour daily searching for documents.**

One of the ways workers can help reduce costs is to follow a standardized set of rules and guidelines for processing records, such as those you are learning now. If records were indexed and coded correctly, they would be easier to locate and fewer records would be misfiled and lost.

Electronic document-management systems help reduce the expense of managing paper by making it easier and more cost-effective to:

- **locate documents.**
- **update documents.**
- **share documents.**
- **store documents.**
- **ensure the security of documents.**

Even with the implementation of systems that convert paper documents to digital form, records can still be difficult to locate when standardized systems are lacking. Electronic records such as e-mail are often disorganized, making searching and retrieving the information unproductive and costly for the organization. Employees would benefit from receiving training on how to best index and manage records. The skills you are now learning will be valuable to any organization.

B. Business Names. Single letters in business and organization names are indexed as written. If single letters are separated by spaces (for example, I C U, X Y Z), index each letter as a separate unit. If single letters are separated by periods (for example, I.B.M., B.S.A.), disregard the periods and index the letters as one unit (IBM, BSA).

Abbreviated words (Co., Inc., Mfg.) and names (CNN, MDA) are indexed as one unit regardless of punctuation or spacing. Acronyms, which are words formed from the first or first few letters of business or organization names, are indexed as one unit regardless of punctuation or spacing (for example, W O W—World Organization of Webmasters, ISTE—International Society for Technology in Education, M.A.D.D.—Mothers Against Drunk Driving). Radio and television station call letters are also indexed as one unit (for example, KKCO, WPRC).

Sometimes it is difficult to tell the difference between a business or organization name that has single letters (A B C, Inc.) and a name that is an acronym (A R C O—Atlantic Richfield Company). When each letter is pronounced separately (as in A B C, Y.M.C.A., or UCLA), the name has single letters and is indexed as written. When the letters are pronounced together as one word (as in A R C O, AMTRAK, or AMOCO), they form an acronym and the name is indexed as one unit.

EXAMPLES: RULE 4B

Name	Key Unit	Unit 2	Unit 3	Unit 4
1. Artists Against A I D S	ARTISTS	AGAINST	AIDS	
2. B G Developers, Inc.	B	G	DEVELOPERS	INC
3. E Z Moving Co.	E	Z	MOVING	CO
4. G & M Supermarket	G	AND	M	SUPERMARKET
5. N A M M	NAMM			
6. N.A.S.D.A.Q.	NASDAQ			
7. The R.A.R. Drive-In	RAR	DRIVEIN	THE	
8. U S B Tours	U	S	B	TOURS
9. West-Side Y.M.C.A.	WESTSIDE	YMCA		
10. WXYZ Television	WXYZ	TELEVISION		

(Indexing Order of Units is the column group header spanning Key Unit through Unit 4.)

CHECK YOUR UNDERSTANDING

Rules 3 and 4   Time Goal: 7 Minutes

Directions: Underline the key indexing unit in each of the following names. Place a small 2 over the second indexing unit, a small 3 over the third indexing unit, and so on. This marking of the units is called **coding.** After you have coded each name, indicate the correct alphabetic order by numbering the names from 1 to 10 in the parentheses provided.

$\overset{2}{}\quad\overset{3}{}$

Example: Dave T. Gonzales

(   ) Patricia Everett-Haynes

(   ) Mama's Home-Style Pies

(   ) R. G. Samuels

(   ) A B C Inc.

(   ) D.R. Home Security

(   ) A-Plus Learning Ctr.

(   ) Toy-a-rama

(   ) Ed's Tile Distr.

(   ) Radio Station KRCW

(   ) A-Z Office Supplies

See page 128 for the correct answers.

Rule 5: Titles and Suffixes

A. Personal Names. A title (Dr., Miss, Mr., Mrs., Ms., Prof.) before a name or a seniority suffix (II, III, Jr., Sr.) or professional suffix (CRM, D.D.S, Mayor, M.D., Ph.D.) after a name is the last indexing unit. Numeric suffixes

(II, III) are filed before alphabetic suffixes (Jr., Mayor, Senator, Sr.). If a name contains both a title and a suffix, the title is the last unit.

Royal and religious titles followed by either a given name (Queen Elizabeth) or a surname only (Father Johnson) are indexed and filed as written.

EXAMPLES: RULE 5A

Name	Key Unit	Unit 2	Unit 3	Unit 4	
		Indexing Order of Units			
1. Tai M. Dang, Ph.D.	DANG	TAI	M	PHD	
2. Lyndsay M. Delafield, D.D.S.	DELAFIELD	LYNDSAY	M	DDS	
3. Mrs. Lyndsay M. Delafield, M.D.	DELAFIELD	LYNDSAY	M	MD	MRS
4. Ramon Delgado	DELGADO	RAMON			
5. Ramon Delgado II	DELGADO	RAMON	II		
6. Ramon Delgado III	DELGADO	RAMON	III		
7. Mr. Ramon P. Delgado	DELGADO	RAMON	P	MR	
8. Raoul Delveccio, Jr.	DELVECCIO	RAOUL	JR		
9. Raoul Delveccio, Sr.	DELVECCIO	RAOUL	SR		
10. Father O'Brian	FATHER	OBRIAN			
11. Mayor Alicia Pridmore	PRIDMORE	ALICIA	MAYOR		
12. Prince William	PRINCE	WILLIAM			

B. Business Names. Titles in business names are indexed as written.

EXAMPLES: RULE 5B

Name	Key Unit	Unit 2	Unit 3	Unit 4
		Indexing Order of Units		
1. Capt. Joe's Camping Gear	CAPT	JOES	CAMPING	GEAR
2. Dr. Kumar's Dental Clinic	DR	KUMARS	DENTAL	CLINIC
3. Mister Yamamoto Gallery	MISTER	YAMAMOTO	GALLERY	
4. Mrs. Youngman Catering	MRS	YOUNGMAN	CATERING	
5. Prof. Hunter Speed-Reading	PROF	HUNTER	SPEEDREADING	
6. Prof. Huong Natural Vitamins	PROF	HUONG	NATURAL	VITAMINS
7. Sondra Silva, CPA, Inc.	SONDRA	SILVA	CPA	INC

Preparing File Cards

You have learned how to apply Rules 1–5 to the names listed in the examples given for each rule. Now you will learn to work with names on cards, as shown in Figure 2-1 on the next page. Follow these steps in preparing cards for filing:

1. **Key or write the name and addresses $1/2$ inch below the line on the card. (Note: The names and addresses are preprinted on the cards you will use to complete the Applications.)**

FIGURE 2-1
File Card

ORTEGA MARIA LILLIAN

2   3
Maria Lillian <u>Ortega</u>
5309 Manchester Drive
San Marcos, CA 92078-0767

2. **Code the name by underlining the key indexing unit and numbering each remaining unit.**
3. **Key or write the name in capital letters and in correct indexing order above the line on the card.**

Preparing Cross-Reference Cards

As you learned in Rules 1–5, each record is filed in original indexing order according to the name. Some names, personal or business, may be referred to in more than one way. Cross-reference cards are prepared showing the alternative names by which a record may be requested. A SEE notation on a cross-reference card indicates the storage location of the original record.

You will prepare cross-reference cards in Practical Application 2A whenever you encounter one of the following situations:

1. **Unusual Names.** When it is difficult to determine the surname, index the name that is in last-name position as the key unit on the original record. Prepare a cross-reference with the first name indexed as the key unit. Examples are *Mr. Alan David* and *Ms. Bau Tran*.

Original Indexing Order	Cross-Reference Order
DAVID ALAN MR	ALAN DAVID MR SEE: DAVID ALAN MR
TRAN BAU MS	BAU TRAN MS SEE: TRAN BAU MS

2. **Hyphenated Surnames.** A cross-reference assists in the retrieval of a record that may be requested by either of the two surnames in a hyphenated surname. Examples are *Bella Flores-Castillo* and *Mr. Hans Fogel-Valle*.

Original Indexing Order	Cross-Reference Order
FLORESCASTILLO BELLA	CASTILLO BELLA FLORES SEE: FLORESCASTILLO BELLA
FOGELVALLE HANS MR	VALLE HANS FOGEL MR SEE: FOGELVALLE HANS MR

3. **Alternative Names.** Prepare a cross-reference when a person is known by more than one name. Examples are *Mrs. Carole Cook,* who is also known as *Mrs. Douglas Cook; TaBetha Hines* aka *Mrs. TaBetha Miller;* and *Mark Twain* aka *Samuel Langhorne Clemens.*

Original Indexing Order	**Cross-Reference Order**
COOK CAROLE MRS	COOK DOUGLAS MRS SEE: COOK CAROLE MRS
HINES TABETHA	MILLER TABETHA MRS SEE: HINES TABETHA
TWAIN MARK	CLEMENS SAMUEL LANGHORNE SEE: TWAIN MARK

4. **Abbreviations and Acronyms.** Although abbreviated business names and acronyms are not written out in full for indexing purposes (see Rule 4B, page 13), they may be referred to by their full names. For that reason, a cross-reference is prepared for the full name. The original record is filed under the abbreviated name. Examples are *STRS (State Teachers Retirement System), AAA (Automobile Association of America),* and *3COM (Computer Communications Company).*

Original Indexing Order	**Cross-Reference Order**
STRS	STATE TEACHERS RETIREMENT SYSTEM SEE: STRS
AAA	AUTOMOBILE ASSOCIATION OF AMERICA SEE: AAA
3COM	COMPUTER COMMUNICATIONS COMPANY SEE: 3COM

5. **Similar Names.** When several names are identical or similar in pronunciation but different in spelling, prepare **SEE ALSO** cross-references under each of the various spellings to aid in the retrieval of the desired record. An example is *Burns,* which can also be spelled *Burnes* or *Byrnes.*

BURNS SEE ALSO: BURNES, BYRNES	BYRNES SEE ALSO: BURNS, BURNES
BURNES SEE ALSO: BYRNES, BURNS	

Follow these steps in preparing cross-reference cards. (See Figure 2-2 on the next page for examples.)

1. On the original card, code the name in the body of the card and write or key the name in capital letters and in correct indexing order at the top of the card.

2. Prepare a second card with the name in cross-reference order written or keyed at the top of the card in all capital letters. Write the original card number and an *X* in the upper right corner. **(Note: Card numbers such as 10 and 10X are used in this text as a way to check your filing order and are not used in an actual office filing system.)**

3. Write or key a SEE notation on the cross-reference card. This notation indicates that the records are filed under the name on the original card.

FIGURE 2-2

Original and Cross-
Reference Cards

Original Cards

Unusual Name

DUONG HOANG DR	10

3   2
Dr. Hoang Duong
8339 Aero Drive
San Diego, CA 92123-1777

Hyphenated Surname

CAPPAROSMATRIANO EVE A MISS	22

4   2   3
Miss Eve A. Capparos-Matriano
1622 East Vista Way
Cleveland, OH 44101-0990

Alternative Name

KANTOR SORAYA MS	11

3   2
Ms. Soraya Kantor (Mrs. Jack Peterson)
37721 S. Highland Avenue
Los Angeles, CA 90036-4321

Abbreviated Name or Acronym

CNN	45

CNN (Cable News Network)
4550 Hollywood Boulevard
Hollywood, CA 90029-1345

Cross-Reference Cards

HOANG DUONG DR	10X

SEE: DUONG HOANG DR

MATRIANO EVE A CAPARROS MISS	22X

SEE: CAPPAROSMATRIANO EVE A MISS

PETERSON JACK MRS	11X

SEE: KANTOR SORAYA MS

CABLE NEWS NETWORK	45X

SEE: CNN

✓

CHECK YOUR UNDERSTANDING

Cross-Referencing   Time Goal: 7 Minutes

Directions: Cross-reference the following five names. First, code each name in original indexing order. Then write the name in cross-reference order on the line provided. Include the SEE notation.

Original	Cross-Reference
2	
Example: Sean Elliott	SEAN ELLIOTT
	SEE: ELLIOTT SEAN
EPCOT	
(Experimental Prototype City of Tomorrow)	SEE:
Mehdi Tazbaz	
	SEE:
Mrs. Juan Bustamonte	
(Mrs. Cecilia Bustamonte)	SEE:
Dr. Shoshana Taylor-Frye	
	SEE:
U.P.S. (United Parcel Service)	
	SEE:

See page 128 for the correct answers.

PRACTICAL APPLICATION 2A
Indexing, Coding, Cross-Referencing, Sorting, and Filing Names on Cards   Time Goal: 1 Hour

Supplies   File box
Cards 1–25 (Forms Pad 1)
8 preprinted guides: C, D, E, F, R, S, T, U (Envelope 1)
4 blank cards for cross-references (Forms Pad 1)
Pencil for coding
Checksheet 2A (Checksheet Packet)
Retrieval Exercise 2A (Checksheet Packet)

Directions

Follow step-by-step.

1. Assemble the file box. This box will serve as both the card file and the correspondence file for use in all Practical Applications. When the pieces are not in use, you may store them inside the box.

2. Place the guides in the file box in alphabetic order.

3. Remove cards 1–25 and the 4 blank cards for cross-references from the forms pad.

4. Code each name on the cards by underlining the key indexing unit and numbering each subsequent unit. (Disregard the number codes; you will use them in a later Practical Application.)

5. Write or key the name in capital letters and in correct indexing order at the top of the card. (Refer to Figure 2-1, page 16.)

6. Prepare cross-reference cards for any unusual names, hyphenated surnames, alternative names, abbreviated names, and acronyms. Review the format for cross-reference cards on pages 16–18.

7. Before filing, sort the 25 cards and 4 cross-reference cards into piles, one for each of the guides C, D, E, F, R, S, and T. (You will have 7 piles. There is no *U* pile for cards 1–25.)

8. File the cards in alphabetic order behind the appropriate guides in the file box.

9. Double-check your filing.

10. Complete Checksheet 2A by recording the numbers of the cards as they are filed in order behind each guide. List the numbers beginning at the bottom of each column. This insures that the numbers will appear in the same order from front to back as do the cards in the file box. Be sure to list cross-references with an *X*. Submit Checksheet 2A to your instructor for checking.

    Here's an example of how to start filling in Checksheet 2A.

4X							
2							
C	D	E	F	R	S	T	U

11. With your instructor's supervision, complete Retrieval Exercise 2A.

12. Keep cards 1–25 and the cross-references in the file box.

Rules for Indexing Personal and Business Names, Continued

Rule 6: Prefixes—Articles and Particles

A foreign article or particle in a personal or business name is combined with the part of the name following it to form a single indexing unit. The indexing order is not affected by a space between a prefix and the rest of the name, and the space is disregarded when indexing. Uppercase and lowercase prefixes are treated the same, and punctuation is omitted.

Examples of articles and particles are *a la, D', Da, De, Del, De la, Della, Den, Des, Di, Dos, Du, E', El, Fitz, Il, L', La, Las, Le, Les, Lo, Los, M', Mac, Me, O', Per, Saint, San, Santa, Santo, St., Ste., Te, Ten, Ter, Van, Van de, Van den, Van der, Von,* and *Von den.*

	Indexing Order of Units			
EXAMPLES: RULE 6				
Name	**Key Unit**	**Unit 2**	**Unit 3**	**Unit 4**
1. A Lá Parisienne Pastries	ALAPARISIENNE	PASTRIES		
2. Lupe de La Fuente, D.D.S.	DELAFUENTE	LUPE	DDS	
3. Ms. Mariah Della Costa	DELLACOSTA	MARIAH	MS	
4. Del Rey Rent-A-Car	DELREY	RENTACAR		
5. D'Vry & Co. Painters	DVRY	AND	CO	PAINTERS
6. Professor Melanie El Hayek	ELHAYEK	MELANIE	PROFESSOR	
7. El Taco del Sol Restaurant	ELTACO	DELSOL	RESTAURANT	
8. Fashion House of San Diego	FASHION	HOUSE	OF	SANDIEGO
9. Il Cielo	ILCIELO			
10. Le Salon de Beaute	LESALON	DEBEAUTE		
11. Mr. Howard Mac Connell	MACCONNELL	HOWARD	MR	
12. Ted McKeon, Sr.	MCKEON	TED	SR	
13. Sister St. James	SISTER	STJAMES		
14. The Van den Berg Studios	VANDENBERG	STUDIOS	THE	
15. Van Nuys Video Mart	VANNUYS	VIDEO	MART	
16. Von Hausen Village	VONHAUSEN	VILLAGE		

Rule 7: Numbers in Business Names

Numbers spelled out in business names (Seven Oaks Spa) are filed alphabetically. Numbers written in digits are filed before alphabetic letters or words. (Century 21 Luggage is filed before Century Twenty-One Loans.) Names with numbers written in digits in the first units are filed in ascending order (lowest to highest number) before alphabetic names (12 Step House, 21 and

Over Club, 65 and up Travel, A Cut Above). Arabic numerals are filed before Roman numerals (2, 3, II, III).

Names with inclusive numbers (20–29) are arranged by the first digit(s) only (20). Names with numbers appearing in other than the first position (Union 76 Station) are filed alphabetically and immediately before a similar name without a number (Union Street Gallery).

When indexing numbers written in digit form that contain *st*, *d*, and *th* (1st, 2d, 3d, 4th), ignore the letter endings and consider only the digits (1, 2, 3, 4).

EXAMPLES: RULE 7

	Indexing Order of Units			
Name	Key Unit	Unit 2	Unit 3	Unit 4
1. 4 Eyes Optometrists, Inc.	4	EYES	OPTOMETRISTS	INC
2. 4th Street Health Club	4	STREET	HEALTH	CLUB
3. 14 Plus Women's Fashions	14	PLUS	WOMENS	FASHIONS
4. 21st Century Devel. Corp.	21	CENTURY	DEVEL	CORP
5. 200–225 Beach Apts.	200	BEACH	APTS	
6. The 2001 Recycling Center	2001	RECYCLING	CENTER	THE
7. VIII Hour Dry Cleaners	VIII	HOUR	DRY	CLEANERS
8. # 1 Philly Cheesesteaks	NUMBER	1	PHILLY	CHEESESTEAKS
9. Number One Auto Service	NUMBER	ONE	AUTO	SERVICE
10. Portrait Gallery 2000	PORTRAIT	GALLERY	2000	
11. Puhol's Restaurant II	PUHOLS	RESTAURANT	II	
12. Ten-Minute Nails	TENMINUTE	NAILS		
13. Tenth Street Coffee Shop	TENTH	STREET	COFFEE	SHOP
14. Twenty-one Club	TWENTYONE	CLUB		
15. Under 25 $ Shoes	UNDER	25	DOLLARS	SHOES
16. Underwood's by-the-Sea	UNDERWOODS	BYTHESEA		

CHECK YOUR UNDERSTANDING

Rules 6 and 7   Time Goal: 10 Minutes

Directions: Determine the key unit and succeeding units in these personal and business names. Write them in all capital letters and in indexing order in the spaces provided. Then alphabetize the names by numbering them from 1 to 10 in the parentheses provided.

Name	Indexing Order of Units			
	Key Unit	Unit 2	Unit 3	Unit 4
( ) T. Shannon Fitz Simmons				
( ) Nasim El Hassanzadeh				
( ) 9 O'Clock Maids				
( ) Ever-Brite Carpet Cleaners No. 9				
( ) San Francisco Deluxe Seafood				
( ) St. Nick's Toys 4 Tots				
( ) 21st Century Airlines				
( ) 9–12 Day Care Serv.				
( ) Santa Barbara Botanical Gardens				
( ) Los Feliz Telecom Corp.				

See page 129 for the correct answers.

Rule 8: Organizations and Institutions

Banks and other financial institutions, clubs, colleges, hospitals, hotels, lodges, magazines, motels, museums, newspapers, religious institutions, schools, unions, universities, and other organizations and institutions are indexed and filed according to the names on their letterheads.

EXAMPLES: RULE 8

Name	Indexing Order of Units			
	Key Unit	Unit 2	Unit 3	Unit 4
1. 1st Internet Bank	1	INTERNET	BANK	
2. American Savings & Loan	AMERICAN	SAVINGS	AND	LOAN
3. The DVD Collectors Club	DVD	COLLECTORS	CLUB	THE
4. Emery State College	EMERY	STATE	COLLEGE	
5. Good Food Magazine	GOOD	FOOD	MAGAZINE	
6. Good Samaritan Hospital	GOOD	SAMARITAN	HOSPITAL	
7. Hotel du Lac	HOTEL	DULAC		
8. Masons Lodge No. IV	MASONS	LODGE	NO	IV
9. Motel 8	MOTEL	8		
10. Natural History Museum	NATURAL	HISTORY	MUSEUM	
11. School of Cosmetology	SCHOOL	OF	COSMETOLOGY	
12. St. Francis Baptist Church	STFRANCIS	BAPTIST	CHURCH	
13. Temple Beth Am	TEMPLE	BETH	AM	
14. Theodore Roosevelt Jr. High	THEODORE	ROOSEVELT	JR	HIGH
15. Troy Sr. High School	TROY	SR	HIGH	SCHOOL
16. Union of Webmasters	UNION	OF	WEBMASTERS	
17. United Teachers of Los Angeles	UNITED	TEACHERS	OF	LOSANGELES
18. University of South Carolina	UNIVERSITY	OF	SOUTH	CAROLINA
19. The Winter Fashion Catalog	WINTER	FASHION	CATALOG	THE

Rule 9: Identical Names

When personal names and names of businesses, institutions, and organizations are exactly the same (including titles as explained in Rule 5), filing order is determined by the addresses. Compare addresses in the following order:

1. **City names**
2. **State or province names (if city names are identical)**
3. **Street names, including *Avenue, Boulevard, Drive, Street*, and so on (if city and state names are identical). Use the following guidelines for determining the order of street names:**
   a. **When the first units of street names are written in digits (8th Avenue), the names are considered in ascending numeric order (1, 2, 3 . . .) and are placed together before alphabetic street names (42d Street, 89th Avenue, Mission Boulevard, Wilshire Boulevard).**

EXAMPLES: RULE 9							
	Indexing Order of Units						
Name	**Key Unit**	**Unit 2**	**Unit 3**	**Unit 4**	**Unit 5**	**Unit 6**	**Unit 7**	**Unit 8**
(Names of cities determine filing order.)								
1. Vanessa Jones Portland, Oregon	JONES	VANESSA	PORTLAND					
2. Vanessa Jones Salem, Oregon	JONES	VANESSA	SALEM					
(Names of states and provinces determine filing order.)								
3. North Lake Theater Bennington, New Hampshire	NORTH	LAKE	THEATER	BENNINGTON	NEW	HAMPSHIRE		
4. North Lake Theater Bennington, Vermont	NORTH	LAKE	THEATER	BENNINGTON	VERMONT			
5. Take-Out Express Victoria, British Columbia	TAKEOUT	EXPRESS	VICTORIA	BRITISH	COLUMBIA			
6. Take-Out Express Victoria, Texas	TAKEOUT	EXPRESS	VICTORIA	TEXAS				
(Names of streets and building numbers determine filing order.)								
7. Honey-Do Handyman Service 890 Beechmont Avenue Cincinnati, OH	HONEYDO	HANDYMAN	SERVICE	CINCINNATI	OHIO	BEECHMONT	AVENUE	890
8. Honey-Do Handyman Service 2289 Main Street Cincinnati, OH	HONEYDO	HANDYMAN	SERVICE	CINCINNATI	OHIO	MAIN	STREET	2289
9. Honey-Do Handyman Service 8004 Main Street Cincinnati, OH	HONEYDO	HANDYMAN	SERVICE	CINCINNATI	OHIO	MAIN	STREET	8004

b. **Street names with compass directions (North, South, East, and West) are considered as written (SE Lincoln Street, South Lincoln Street). Street names written as digits after compass directions are considered before alphabetic street names:**

East 17th

East Rushmore Way

SE 30th

SE Sixth

Southeast Sixth

4. **House or building numbers (if city, state, and street names are identical). Use the following guidelines for determining the order of house or building numbers:**

   a. **House and building numbers written as digits are considered in ascending numeric order (5 Corinth Towers, 216 Corinth Towers) and placed together before alphabetic building names (The Corinth Towers).**

   b. **When both a street address and a building name are in an address, disregard the building name.**

   c. **ZIP Codes are not considered in determining filing order.**

Rule 10: Government Names

Government names are indexed first by the name of the governmental unit—country, state, county, or city. The distinctive name of the department, bureau, office, or board is indexed next. The words *Office of, Department of, Bureau of,* and so on, are separate indexing units when they are part of the official name.

(**Note:** If *of* or *of the* is not part of the official name as written, it is enclosed in parentheses and not considered.)

A. Federal. The first indexing unit of a U.S. (federal) government agency name is *United States Government.*

EXAMPLES: RULE 10A	
Name	**Indexed Order**
1. U.S. Army Department Reserve Training Center	UNITED STATES GOVERNMENT ARMY DEPARTMENT RESERVE TRAINING CENTER
2. U.S. Department of State Passport Agency	UNITED STATES GOVERNMENT STATE DEPARTMENT (OF) PASSPORT AGENCY
3. U.S. Department of the Treasury Internal Revenue Service	UNITED STATES GOVERNMENT TREASURY DEPARTMENT (OF THE) INTERNAL REVENUE SERVICE

B. State and Local. The first indexing unit is the name of the state, province, county, parish, city, town, township, or village. The next indexing unit is the most distinctive name of the department, board, bureau, office, or government/political division. When they are part of the official name, the words *State of,* *County of,* *Department of,* and *Board of* are considered separate indexing units.

EXAMPLES: RULE 10B	
Name	**Indexed Order**
1. State of California Highway Patrol	CALIFORNIA STATE OF HIGHWAY PATROL
2. District of Columbia Athletic Commission	COLUMBIA DISTRICT OF ATHLETIC COMMISSION
3. County of Los Angeles Fire Department	LOSANGELES COUNTY OF FIRE DEPARTMENT
4. City of Peoria Mayor's Office	PEORIA CITY OF MAYORS OFFICE
5. Tampa Public Social Services Department	TAMPA PUBLIC SOCIAL SERVICES DEPARTMENT

C. Foreign. The distinctive translated English name is the first indexing unit for a foreign government name. This is followed, if needed and if part of the official name, by the remainder of the formal name of the government. Branches, departments, and divisions follow in order by their distinctive translated names. States, colonies, provinces, cities, and other divisions of foreign governments are filed by their official names as spelled in English. If necessary, prepare a cross-reference for the original foreign spelling of the name. (See cross-reference examples on page 30.)

EXAMPLES: RULE 10C	
Name	**Indexed Order**
1. Federative Republic of Brazil	BRAZIL FEDERATIVE REPUBLIC OF
2. Republic of India	INDIA REPUBLIC OF
3. Eire	IRELAND
4. Democratic People's Republic of Korea	KOREA DEMOCRATIC PEOPLES REPUBLIC OF
5. Dawlat Al Amarat al Arabiyah al Muttahidah	UNITED ARAB EMIRATES
6. Estados Unidos Mexicanos	UNITED MEXICAN STATES

Note: The *United States Government Manual* and the *Congressional Directory,* both published annually, report a current list of U.S. government agencies and offices. Those publications are available online at the U.S. Government Printing Office web site: http://www.gpoaccess.gov/databases.html. *Countries, Dependencies, Areas of Special Sovereignty, and Their Principal Administrative Divisions* is a Federal Information Processing Standards Publication (FIPS PUB) issued by the National Institute of Standards and

Technology after being approved by the Secretary of Commerce. This publication provides a list of geographic and political entities of the world and associated standard codes. This publication is available from the FIPS web site at http://www.itl.nist.gov/fipspubs/fip10-4.htm. The *World Almanac and Book of Facts*, updated annually, includes facts and statistics on many foreign nations and is helpful as a source of English spellings for many foreign names.

CHECK YOUR UNDERSTANDING

Rules 8, 9, and 10   Time Goal: 12 Minutes

Part 1

Directions: Are the names in each pair in alphabetic order? Indicate in the space provided whether the correct order is *ab* or *ba*.

_____1. a. Trek Blue Software, Arcadia, Pennsylvania
            b. Trek Blue Software, Arcadia, California
_____2. a. Mrs. Sureli Patel, Winston, Wyoming
            b. Mrs. Sureli Patel, Winston-Salem, North Carolina
_____3. a. Flower Mart, 11 Meade Road, Seattle, Washington
            b. Flower Mart, 342 Orchard Drive, Seattle, Washington
_____4. a. Megan Andrews, Ph.D., 6580 Tenth Street, Newark, New Jersey
            b. Megan Andrews, Ph.D., 6880 21st Street, Newark, New Jersey
_____5. a. Utility Skateboards, Inc., 772 East 5th Avenue, Salt Lake City, Utah
            b. Utility Skateboards, Inc., 9221 East 5th Avenue, Salt Lake City, Utah

Part 2

Directions: Code each of the following 10 names by underlining the key indexing unit and numbering the succeeding units. Then alphabetize the names by numbering them from 1 to 10 in the parentheses provided.

                                    2
Example: <u>St. Mark's</u> Cathedral

(   ) Martin Luther King, Jr., High School
(   ) Sylvan City Motel
(   ) Society of Marriage & Family Counselors
(   ) University of Pennsylvania
(   ) U.S. Office of Management and Budget
(   ) U.S. National Aeronautics & Space Administration
(   ) Foreign Exchange Office, Treasury Department, Kingdom of Norway
(   ) Pensacola Department of Public Housing
(   ) 1st Federal Savings & Investments
(   ) United Financial Services

See page 129 for the correct answers.

Cross-Referencing Business Names

Cross-references should be prepared for the following types of business names. The original name is the name appearing on the company letterhead.

1. **Compound Names.** When a business name includes two or more surnames, file the original card or record under the surname listed first and prepare a cross-reference for each surname other than the first.

   Example: *Taylor and Yang, Inc.*

   File the original under *Taylor.* Prepare a cross-reference under *Yang.*

   Example: *Kendall, Adigun, and Martinez, Inc.*

   File the original under *Kendall.* Prepare cross-references for both *Adigun* and *Martinez* by completing the following steps:

   a. Write or key the name in capital letters and in indexing order at the top of the original card as shown in Figure 2-3.

FIGURE 2-3
Card 1
(Original Card)

KENDALL ADIGUN AND MARTINEZ INC   I

Kendall, Adigun, and Martinez, Inc.
4042 Crest Avenue
Madison, WI 53703-4042

   b. Rearrange the original name in a rotation manner and write or key it at the top of the cross-reference card as shown in Figure 2-4. The original order of the name follows the SEE notation.

FIGURE 2-4
Card 2
(Cross-Reference Card)

Kendall Adigun and Martinez Inc

ADIGUN MARTINEZ AND KENDALL INC   IX

SEE: KENDALL ADIGUN AND MARTINEZ INC

   c. Rotate the names again as shown in Figure 2-5.

FIGURE 2-5

Card 3
(Cross-Reference Card)

Adigun Martinez and Kendall Inc

MARTINEZ KENDALL AND ADIGUN INC   IX

SEE: KENDALL ADIGUN AND MARTINEZ INC

Question: What is the alphabetic order of those three cards?
Answer: First: ADIGUN MARTINEZ AND KENDALL INC   IX
                Second: KENDALL ADIGUN AND MARTINEZ INC   I
                Third: MARTINEZ KENDALL AND ADIGUN INC   IX

2. **Abbreviations and Acronyms.** Review the discussion of cross-referencing abbreviations and acronyms on page 17 and review Figure 2-2 on page 18.

3. **Popular and Coined Names.** A business is often known by its popular and/or coined name. File by the most commonly used name or title and cross-reference under the full name of the business. Examples are *Herschel's* (Herschel's Bakery and Deli) and *BMW* (Bavarian Motor Works).

Original Indexing Order	Cross-Reference Order
HERSCHELS	HERSCHELS BAKERY AND DELI SEE: HERSCHELS
BMW	BAVARIAN MOTOR WORKS SEE: BMW

4. **Hyphenated Names.** As with personal names, business names with hyphens require a cross-reference. Examples are *Alavi-Fox Mortgage Brokers* and *Brite-Smile Dental Center.*

Original Indexing Order	Cross-Reference Order
ALAVIFOX MORTGAGE BROKERS	FOXALAVI MORTGAGE BROKERS SEE: ALAVIFOX MORTGAGE BROKERS
BRITESMILE DENTAL CENTER	SMILEBRITE DENTAL CENTER SEE: BRITESMILE DENTAL CENTER

5. **Divisions and Subsidiaries.** A business may have its own name, but it may actually be a division or subsidiary of another company. Examples are *Star Software*, a subsidiary of Galaxy Enterprises, Inc., and *InfoWorld*, a division of Treo Publishers.

Original Indexing Order	Cross-Reference Order
STAR SOFTWARE	GALAXY ENTERPRISES INC SEE: STAR SOFTWARE
INFOWORLD	TREO PUBLISHERS SEE: INFOWORLD

6. **Changed Names.** If a company changes its name, file the original under the new name. An example is *Syllabus.com* that changed its name to *Campus Technology.com.*

Original Indexing Order	Cross-Reference Order
CAMPUS TECHNOLOGYCOM	SYLLABUSCOM SEE: CAMPUS TECHNOLOGYCOM

7. **Similar Names.** Similar names for a business include examples such as CheckPoint or Check Point, Southwest or South West, and All State or All-state. Names that could be considered as one or two units are good candidates for cross-references. A SEE ALSO cross-reference is prepared to inform of other possible spellings. The complete business name is not cross-referenced—only the similar name. Examples are *AirTek Environmental Systems* and *Goodwill Industries.*

Original Indexing Order	Cross-Reference Order
AIRTEK ENVIRONMENTAL SYSTEMS	AIR TEK SEE ALSO: AIRTEK
GOODWILL INDUSTRIES	GOOD WILL SEE ALSO: GOODWILL

8. **Non-English Business Names.** File the original under the English spelling of the business name and cross-reference the non-English spelling. Examples are *LeLycée Francais De Los Angeles* and *Para Los Ninos.*

Original Indexing Order	Cross-Reference Order
FRENCH HIGH SCHOOL OF LOSANGELES THE	LELYCEE FRANCAIS DE LOS ANGELES SEE: FRENCH HIGH SCHOOL OF LOS ANGELES THE
FOR THE CHILDREN	PARA LOSNINOS SEE: FOR THE CHILDREN

9. **Foreign Government Names.** File the original under the English spelling of the government name and cross-reference the foreign spelling. An example is *Republica Federativa do Brasil Secretario de Educação Publica.*

Original Indexing Order	Cross-Reference Order
BRAZIL FEDERATIVE REPUBLIC OF PUBLIC EDUCATION SECRETARY OF	REPUBLICA FEDERATIVA DOBRASIL SECRETARIO DEEDUCACAO PUBLICA SEE: BRAZIL FEDERATIVE REPUBLIC OF PUBLIC EDUCATION SECRETARY OF

CHECK YOUR UNDERSTANDING

Cross-Referencing Business Names   Time Goal: 7 Minutes

Directions: Cross-reference the following five names. First, code each name in original indexing order. Then write the name in cross-reference order on the line provided. Include the SEE notation.

Original	Cross-Reference
2 3 4	
Example: <u>Katz</u> and Sorkin Co.	SORKIN AND KATZ CO SEE: KATZ AND SORKIN CO

Manwani and Mazin Architects

SEE: _____

Aquarius Scuba Equipment
(Subsidiary of Sports Gear, Inc.)   SEE: _____

Viejas
(Viejas Family Fun Center)   SEE: _____

Vantage-Crystal Wireless

SEE: _____

PacTel
(Pacific Telephone Co.)   SEE: _____

See page 130 for the correct answers.

PRACTICAL APPLICATION 2B
Indexing, Coding, Cross-Referencing, Sorting, and Interfiling Names on Cards

Time Goal: 1 Hour

Supplies   File box containing cards 1–25 already filed
Cards 26–50 (Forms Pad 2)
1 preprinted guide: NAMES WITH NUMBERS (Envelope 1)
3 blank cards for cross-references (Forms Pad 1)
Pencil for coding
Checksheet 2B (Checksheet Packet)
Retrieval Exercise 2B (Checksheet Packet)

Directions
Follow step-by-step.

1. **Place the NAMES WITH NUMBERS guide in front of the C guide in the file box.**

2. **Remove cards 26–50 and 3 blank cards from the forms pads.**

3. **Code each name. Then write or key it in capital letters and in correct indexing order at the top of the card.**

4. **Prepare cross-reference cards as needed.**

5. **Before filing, sort cards 26–50 and the 3 cross-reference cards into piles, one for each guide: NAMES WITH NUMBERS, C, D, E, F, R, S, T, and U.**

6. **Interfile those cards in alphabetic order with the cards you filed in Practical Application 2A.**

7. **Double-check your filing.**

8. **Complete Checksheet 2B and give it to your instructor for checking. Make sure you list the card numbers beginning at the bottom of each column.**

9. With your instructor's supervision, complete Retrieval Exercise 2B.

10. Remove all cards and guides from the file box. Store the guides in Envelope 1 for reuse. Discard the cross-reference cards. Arrange the cards in numeric order from 1–50. Cards 1–25 will be used in Chapter 4 for Practical Application 4B. Cards 1–50 will be used in Computer Applications 2A and 2B.

COMPUTER APPLICATION 2A (SEE APPENDIX A.)
Opening and Defining a Table, Adding Records, and Printing a Report

COMPUTER APPLICATION 2B (SEE APPENDIX A.)
Adding Records, Sorting Alphabetically, and Printing a Report

End-of-Chapter Activity

Team up with another classmate. Interview someone who works in a business or medical office. Conduct your interview over the phone, in person, or via e-mail. Ask at least three of the following questions and two questions of your own, for a total of five interview questions. Share the interviewee's answers with the class.

1. **What types of records do you have in your organization?**

2. **Do you have a centralized records department, or do individual departments maintain their own records?**

3. Do you have a paper-based, computerized, or combination system for managing records? Please describe the system that you use.

4. What is your level of familiarity with ARMA's indexing rules, or does your organization have a standardized set of indexing rules?

5. Does your organization have a policy or set of guidelines for how long to keep incoming and outgoing e-mails? If so, please describe it.

Chapter 3: Alphabetic Filing Procedures

Learning Goals

- Perform the six steps involved in processing correspondence and other documents.
- Index records for key words.
- Process requests to charge out records.
- Color-code names in an alphabetic file.

Introduction

Now that you have practiced indexing, coding, cross-referencing, and filing names, you are ready to expand your knowledge of alphabetic filing procedures by working with a variety of office documents. Although every office maintains a unique set of paper-based and electronic records, understanding how to manage records in general is important.

This chapter presents the six steps involved in processing correspondence, forms, financial reports, and other office documents. Four Practical Applications give you experience in applying the rules for filing personal and business names, learning to index records for key words, and processing requests to borrow records from your file. The section on color-coding alphabetic files describes how to apply a color-coding system to names in an alphabetic file.

Alphabetic Correspondence Filing Procedures

Refer to the upcoming Figure 3-1 as you study the sections explaining the six steps involved in alphabetic correspondence filing. The six steps for processing correspondence and other documents are inspecting, indexing, cross-referencing, coding, sorting, and filing.

Step 1: Inspecting

Inspecting means making sure that a record has been released for filing. Before filing any record, you must be certain that someone in your office has completed what needs to be done with the record. You are responsible for checking whether the record has been released (approved) for filing. When a record is ready to be filed, it will have a **release mark,** such as the initials of the person who processed it, somewhere on the record.

FIGURE 3-1
Letter Properly Released
and Coded

²   ³
LTP of America
499 E. Olympic Boulevard
Los Angeles, CA 90015-1806
(310) 555-9792

July 29, ----

Mr. Carter Mahmoudi   AUG 2, ----, 10:30 a.m.
Vice President, Programs
The Learning Zone, Inc.
42260 El Camino Real
San Diego, CA 92121-4226

Dear Mr. Mahmoudi:

²   ³   ⁴   ⁵
The Leadership Training Program of America is planning a Career Day Event   X
for Los Angeles area high school juniors and seniors, and we are inviting you
to attend. Students will benefit from learning firsthand about how you started
your career as a young entrepreneur and then built a successful company. We
are also interested in learning more about the important community service
programs of The Learning Zone.

The Career Day Event will be held on the last Saturday of September at 9 a.m.
Would you be available to give a 20-minute presentation about your recycling
and worldwide conservation programs and your career advice to an audience
of approximately 75 students and parents? Please call my office and let my
assistant know whether you will be able to participate in the Career Day Event.
I certainly hope you can make it!

Sincerely,

Mike Yamamoto

Mike Yamamoto
Executive Director

lh

CM

Look for the release mark on the letter to Carter Mahmoudi in Figure 3-1.
You should find the initials *CM*. Release marks might be formatted in one or
more of the following styles:

- **A person's initials.** This type of release mark is commonly used in offices.
- **The words *Tickler, Pending, Follow-Up,* or *Future Use* and a date.**
  For example, *Tickler 12/11/----* means that the records manager is to
  retrieve the record from the file on December 11 of the designated year.
  The records manager keeps a date file (tickler file) on index cards or in
  the computer and checks it daily. Behind each daily guide is a list of the
  records that are to be retrieved that day, the name of the person in the
  office who made the tickler request, and the action that is to be taken.
- **The words *Form Letter Sent* or *Reply Sent* and a date.** These nota-
  tions indicate that action was taken in response to a piece of correspon-
  dence by a form letter or another form of reply.

If you do not see a release mark, ask the person responsible for the record
if the record is ready for filing.

Notice that the letter in Figure 3-1 also contains a stamped date and time, *AUG 2, ----, 10:30 a.m.* This date is stamped on the letter when it is received by your office and should not be confused with the actual date of the letter, July 29, ----.

Step 2: Indexing

Remember that **indexing** is selecting the name under which a record will be filed—the **filing segment.** The indexing process used for correspondence depends on whether the items are incoming or outgoing.

Incoming Correspondence. Read each piece of correspondence. A quick reading will ensure that you select the correct name for indexing. Learn these four rules for indexing incoming correspondence:

1. **Keep in mind that the record should be filed under the most important name, that is, the name most likely to be used when retrieving the record.**

2. **The name on the letterhead is usually the most important name. If the incoming correspondence is on plain paper instead of letterhead, index the name in the signature line.**

3. **When both the company name on the letterhead and the name in the signature line are important, index the company name.**

4. **Make sure the letterhead is related to the correspondence. Sometimes people use a company letterhead for unrelated matters. For example, a personal business letter may be written on hotel stationery. If that is the case, index the name in the signature line.**

CHECK YOUR UNDERSTANDING

Rules 1–4 for Incoming Correspondence   Time Goal: 2 Minutes

Directions: Write your answer on the line provided below each question.

1. **Read the letter (incoming correspondence) in Figure 3-1. What name should be indexed? Code the name.**

   _____

2. **If the letter in Figure 3-1 were on plain paper instead of letterhead, what name would you index? Code the name.**

   _____

See page 130 for the correct answers.

Outgoing Correspondence. In today's offices, outgoing correspondence is often prepared with word processing software and stored in a computer. Many offices file paper photocopies, or **hard copies,** of outgoing correspondence. In the Practical Applications, the stamp COPY marks copies of outgoing correspondence. A hard copy of an outgoing fax is also considered outgoing correspondence.

As with incoming documents, the first step in the indexing process is to read the correspondence to make sure you select the correct name for indexing. Remember these two points about indexing outgoing correspondence:

1. **The name of the person or company to whom the correspondence has been sent is found in the inside address. When both a company name and a person's name are in the inside address, index the company name.**

2. **Copies of outgoing correspondence do not need release marks; they are ready to be processed and filed.**

Step 3: Cross-Referencing

When indexing both incoming and outgoing correspondence, you may find more than one important name. In addition to the name on the letterhead or in the inside address, you may find that the body of the letter contains another important name. If that record might be requested by more than one name, prepare a cross-reference.

In Chapter 2, you learned the types of names that need to be cross-referenced:

- **Unusual names (page 16)**
- **Hyphenated surnames (page 16)**
- **Alternative names (page 17)**
- **Abbreviations and acronyms (page 17)**
- **Similar names (page 17)**
- **Compound business names (page 28)**
- **Popular and coined names (page 29)**
- **Hyphenated business names (page 29)**
- **Divisions and subsidiaries (page 29)**
- **Changed names (page 29)**
- **Similar business names (page 30)**
- **Non-English business names (page 30)**
- **Foreign government names (page 30)**

When those types of names appear in correspondence, they are usually cross-referenced. Cross-reference the names the first time they appear only. Subsequent correspondence to or from the same correspondent does not require another cross-reference. The procedure for preparing cross-reference sheets is explained in the next section.

Step 4: Coding

You will recall that **coding** is marking the name or subject under which a record will be filed. Coding saves time in the long run because when papers are retrieved, refiling is faster and more accurate when coding marks are on the record. You coded the names on cards in Chapter 2, and you will follow a similar procedure for correspondence.

Look at the letter in Figure 3-1, shown previously. The name on the letterhead, *LTP of America,* is the most important name. Remember that abbreviations are indexed as written. Code the name by underlining the key unit, *LTP,* and numbering the subsequent units.

FIGURE 3-2

Cross-Reference Sheet

CROSS-REFERENCE SHEET

Name or Subject <u>LEADERSHIP TRAINING PROGRAM OF AMERICA</u>
                                        2   3   4   5

Address <u>499 E. Olympic Boulevard</u>

<u>Los Angeles, CA 90015-1806</u>

Date of Record <u>July 29, ----</u>
Brief Summary <u>Career Day Presentation by Carter Mahmoudi</u>

SEE   <u>LTP OF AMERICA</u>

<u>499 E. Olympic Boulevard</u>

<u>Los Angeles, CA 90015-1806</u>

Ramona Hendricks   *August 4, ----*
Records Manager   Date

Did you notice that *LTP of America* needs a cross-reference under the full name as written in the first paragraph? This organization might be referred to as *Leadership Training Program of America.* Code the cross-reference by placing a wavy line under the key unit, *Leadership,* and numbering the subsequent units. Remember to include the words *of America* as part of the cross-referenced name. Also place an X in the right margin as a reminder to prepare a cross-reference.

The records manager prepares cross-reference sheets, as shown in Figure 3-2, that are placed in the correspondence file. Notice the following:

1. ***Leadership Training Program of America* is coded in cross-reference form by placing a wavy line under the key unit and numbering the succeeding units.**

2. **The records manager, Ramona Hendricks, has filled out the *Address, Date of Record, Brief Summary,* and *SEE* sections and has signed and dated the cross-reference sheet.**

FIGURE 3-3
Coded Correspondence
with Cross-Reference
Notation

```
                    2        3        4
             Williams & Coleman, Inc.
                  7331 Venice Boulevard
                 Los Angeles, CA 90023-0021

                                    2        3       4
                      COLEMAN AND WILLIAMS INC   X


        September 27, ----

                                              REC'D SEPT 30, ----


        New Life-Styles Magazine
        586 Garfield Avenue
        Seattle, WA 98101-4407

        Ladies and Gentlemen:

        Enclosed is our bid for updating the web site of New Life-Styles magazine. This bid
        reflects a careful study of the project by our experienced web design team, and we
        believe it to be the most reasonable estimate possible.

        We would appreciate hearing from you as soon as you have reached a
        decision.

        Sincerely yours,

        Estella Santos

        Estella Santos
        Web Project Manager

        js

        Enclosure




                                                         cg
```

Question:	Alphabetically, which would come first, the letter or the cross-reference sheet?
Answer:	The cross-reference sheet would come first because Leadership comes before LTP.

The name to be cross-referenced may be on the letterhead (as in the case of compound names), as shown in Figure 3-3. In this case, rewrite the name in cross-reference form near the letterhead, code it (a wavy line under the key unit, subsequent units numbered), and place an *X* in the right margin.

Step 5: Sorting

To save filing time, sort items to be filed into alphabetic piles as you did in Practical Applications 2A and 2B. Put all pieces of correspondence having key units starting with *C* together, all pieces having key units starting with *D*

WORKPLACE FOCUS

Scanning Paper Records

Many businesses are considering scanning paper documents to increase the security of records and access to information, as well as to reduce the amount of equipment and storage space needed for paper records. Also known as **document imaging**, the task of converting paper records to digital format has benefits as well as drawbacks. After careful analysis of their needs, many organizations decide to hire an outside company to perform the conversion because of the expertise and high-quality scanning hardware offered by document imaging vendors.

The following issues need to be examined within an organization before a system of scanning paper records is implemented:

- **What are the business objectives for scanning records?**
- **Is there a requirement for the documents to be shared within the office? Will scanning meet this requirement?**

- **What file format should be used?**
- **What are the standards for image quality?**
- **Where will the electronic files be stored?**
- **Who will have access to the electronic files?**
- **Should the original paper records be kept?**
- **When and how will the electronic files be disposed of when they are no longer required?**

If those issues are not examined prior to beginning the paper-to-digital conversion, the scanning project has the potential for failure. The bottom line for an organization is to make sure that it has developed sound records management policies and procedures and that those policies are the foundation for implementing any new technology for managing records.

together, and so on. If 10 or more pieces accumulate in one pile, arrange those pieces in alphabetic order before filing them. Work smarter, not harder.

Step 6: Filing

Follow the alphabetic filing rules in Chapter 2. Remember, misfiling wastes time and money. Here are three helpful records management tips:

1. **Place all papers in the file folders with their letterheads or tops to the left, printed side facing you (or frontward). When a file folder is removed from the file and opened, the papers inside should appear in reading position.**
2. **Remove paper clips. If pages must be attached, staple them together in the upper right corner to prevent other papers from being inserted between them.**
3. **File correspondence in either individual or general folders, as described next.**

Study Figure 3-4 to become familiar with the names of the filing supplies used in alphabetic filing.

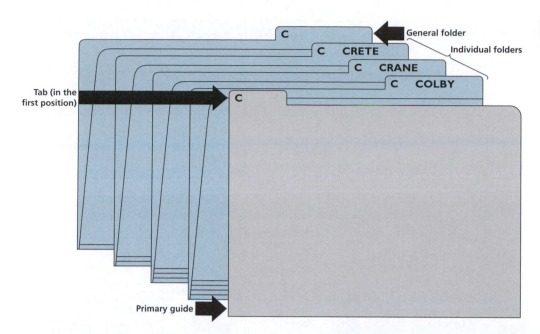

FIGURE 3-4
Alphabetic Filing Supplies

Individual Folders. When three or more pieces of correspondence pertaining to the same person or business accumulate, they are filed in an individual folder. Within the individual folder, file according to the date of the item; the most recent item is always placed on top (in front).

General Folders. In each alphabetic section of the file, a general folder is placed behind the individual folders and is used to store items that do not require an individual folder. Items within the general folders are filed alphabetically. If two pieces pertain to the same correspondent, file the most recent one in front of the earlier one.

Background Information for Practical Applications in Chapters 3–6

BEST PRACTICES

Using PDF Technology

A popular file format used for scanned documents is called PDF.

- PDF stands for Portable Document Format.
- The software for reading PDF files is available free from Adobe Acrobat.
- PDF files are compatible with both Macs and PCs.
- PDF files are an inexpensive way to make documents accessible on the Web.
- PDF reduces the file size of large documents.
- PDF files are highly resistant to viruses.
- PDF documents are secure from content being changed or copied.

You are the records manager for The Learning Zone, Inc., 42260 E1 Camino Real, San Diego, CA 92121-4226. The Learning Zone is a company of 350 employees that was started five years ago by a group of students at the University of San Diego as a senior summer project. They wanted to help solve environmental problems and promote community recycling projects. The company has grown to include conservation projects around the world, educational workshops, research projects for improving recycling and reducing air and water pollution, and development of computer software programs and computer games with an environmental theme. The Learning Zone operates an on-site day-care center for children of employees and for children who live in the community.

FIGURE 3-5

The Learning Zone, Inc., Organization Chart

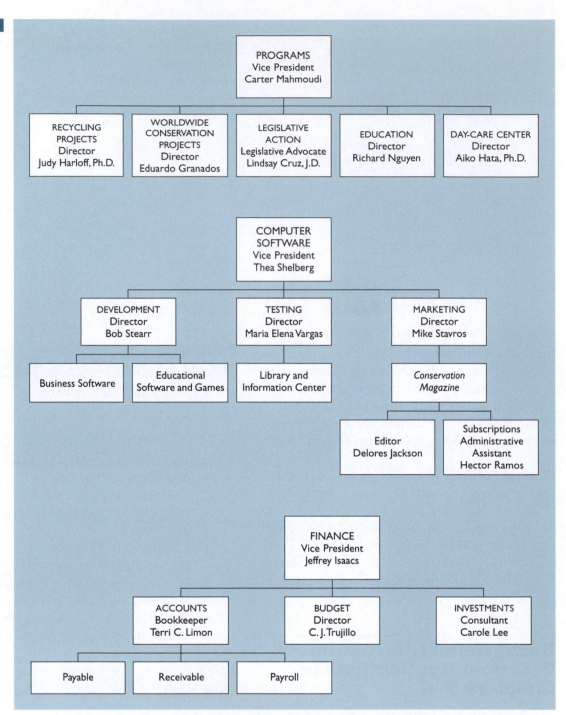

The Learning Zone has three main divisions: Programs, Computer Software, and Finance. Each of the three main divisions has a vice president. See Figure 3-5 for The Learning Zone organization chart.

The Programs Division has five departments: Recycling Projects, Worldwide Conservation Projects, Legislative Action, Education, and the Day-Care Center. The Computer Software Division is divided into three departments: Development, Testing, and Marketing. The Finance Division is also divided into three departments: Accounts, Budget, and Investments. The names of the people who supervise those departments are shown on the organization chart.

As records manager for The Learning Zone, your job is to maintain the files in the records center for all three divisions and their departments.

PRACTICAL APPLICATION 3A
Alphabetic Correspondence Filing
of Personal and Business Names   Time Goal: 1 Hour

Supplies   File box
Correspondence pieces 1–15 (Forms Pad 3)
1 cross-reference sheet (Forms Pad 3)
5 previously used preprinted guides: NAMES WITH NUMBERS,
   C, D, E, F (Envelope 1)
5 preprinted general folders: NAMES WITH NUMBERS, C, D,
   E, F (Envelope 2)
2 unprinted individual folders (Envelope 3)
2 white labels (Envelope 1):

      D   DELMAR CREATIVE GRAPHICS
      F   FIVESTAR TOURS AND TRAVEL

Checksheet 3A (Checksheet Packet)

Directions
Follow step-by-step.

1. **Set up the correspondence file with the guides and general folders
   shown in the following illustration. Keep the individual folders separate
   until you are ready to sort and file the correspondence (step 4).**

2. **Remove correspondence pieces 1–15 and the cross-reference sheet from
   the forms pad.**

3. **For pieces 1–15, follow the Inspecting, Indexing, Cross-Referencing, and
   Coding steps on pages 34–39. Cross-reference one record, piece 9. Be
   sure to write the number of the record and an *X* in the space provided at
   the bottom of the cross-reference sheets. Piece 8 is an incoming fax, and
   piece 11 is an outgoing fax; process them as you would incoming and
   outgoing correspondence.**

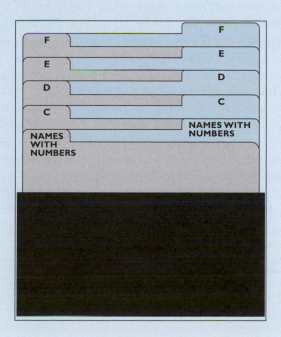

4. After you have coded and cross-referenced all 15 pieces, follow the Sorting and Filing steps on pages 39–41. Place the two white labels on the unprinted folders to create two individual folders. File the appropriate pieces in each individual folder. Then place each individual folder behind its corresponding alphabetic guide. (Refer to Figure 3-4.) Return the sheet of labels to Envelope 1.

5. Complete Checksheet 3A and give it to your instructor for checking.

6. Keep your file box as it is; you will be using it in Practical Application 3B to interfile additional records.

Filing Forms Alphabetically

In addition to correspondence, records managers often work with other paper documents—such as invoices, resumes, application forms, minutes, and spreadsheets—and with microforms, such as microfiche. Study the following procedures for filing forms alphabetically. Filing these kinds of records will provide you with a wider variety of records management experience and give you some familiarity with how these records are handled. Be aware that each office will have its own procedures for filing these types of forms.

Note: The records referenced in parentheses at the end of each procedure are records from the Practical Applications indicated. These records are examples of the forms described. When you work through Practical Application 3B, refer to the following filing procedures for the records indicated.

- **Application Forms.** Application forms for enrollment in The Learning Zone Day-Care Center are filed under the name of the child. Be sure to inspect the application form for a release mark in the form of the word *FILE.* Prepare a cross-reference sheet under the name of the parent filling out the application form. (Record 30 in Practical Application 3B)

- **Faxes.** Correspondence is often sent to The Learning Zone via fax from the sender's computer or fax machine to the fax machine at The Learning Zone. Incoming faxed correspondence is filed according to the rules for incoming correspondence on page 36. Outgoing faxes sent from The Learning Zone are filed according to the rules for outgoing correspondence on pages 36–37. (Records 8 and 11 in Practical Application 3A)

- **Invoices.** Invoices are forms listing information such as items sold, quantity, price, method of shipment, invoice number, and date of sale. Invoices received by The Learning Zone for goods that the company has purchased are paid by the accounts department. A copy of each invoice is sent to you for filing after it has been paid. Follow these steps:

  1. Inspect the invoice for a release mark in the form of the word *PAID* and a date.

  2. Because The Learning Zone receives only a few invoices, file them under the sender's name. In some offices, invoices are filed numerically according to the invoice number. (Record 16 in Practical Application 3B)

- **Minutes.** The Learning Zone keeps a written record of each board of directors meeting in the form of minutes. Copies of the minutes are sent to each member of the board, and one copy is retained in the files under the name *Caldano & de la Cruz, Attorneys-At-Law,* who chair the board. **(Record 20 in Practical Application 3B)**

- **Resumes.** File the resumes of candidates for positions on the staff of The Learning Zone after you check for the release mark *FILE.* Resumes are filed under the candidate's name. **(Record 28 in Practical Application 3B)**

- **Spreadsheets.** Spreadsheets are records that contain numeric information in a worksheet or table format. The Learning Zone receives financial documents, such as year-end financial statements, in spreadsheet form from its accountant. File these under the name of the accounting firm after you check for the release mark *FILE.* **(Record 23 in Practical Application 3B)**

CHECK YOUR UNDERSTANDING

Filing Microfiche Alphabetically   Time Goal: 2 Minutes

Directions: The microfiche below are to be refiled in the microfiche holder shown to the right. Indicate the correct alphabetic order of the 10 microfiche (according to their captions) by numbering them from 1 to 10 in the parentheses provided.

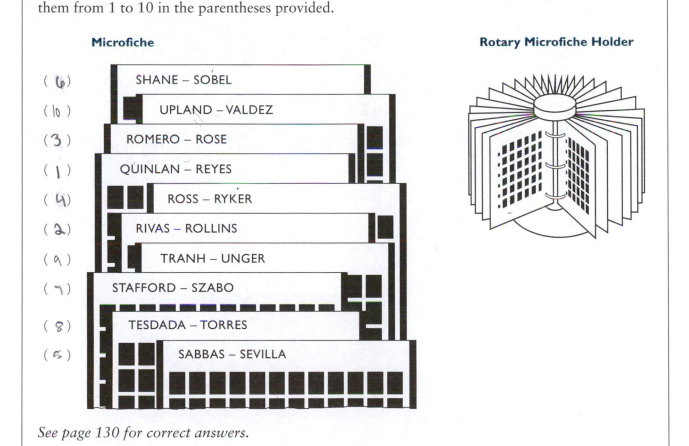

Microfiche   Rotary Microfiche Holder

(6) SHANE – SOBEL

(10) UPLAND – VALDEZ

(3) ROMERO – ROSE

(1) QUINLAN – REYES

(4) ROSS – RYKER

(2) RIVAS – ROLLINS

(9) TRANH – UNGER

(7) STAFFORD – SZABO

(8) TESDADA – TORRES

(5) SABBAS – SEVILLA

See page 130 for correct answers.

PRACTICAL APPLICATION 3B
Alphabetic Correspondence and Forms
Filing of Personal and Business Names   Time Goal: 1 Hour

Supplies   File box containing correspondence pieces 1–15 already filed
Correspondence and forms pieces 16–30 (Forms Pad 3)
1 cross-reference sheet (Forms Pad 3)
4 previously used preprinted guides: R, S, T, U (Envelope 1)
4 preprinted general folders: R, S, T, U (Envelope 2)
2 new unprinted individual folders (Envelope 3)
2 white labels (Envelope 1):
     C   CALDANO AND DELACRUZ ATTORNEYS
             AT LAW
     D   DARTT UNIVERSITY
Checksheet 3B (Checksheet Packet)
Retrieval Exercise 3B (Checksheet Practice)

Directions
Follow step-by-step.

1. **Add the four guides and four general folders to your file so it looks like the following illustration. Keep the two new individual folders separate until you are ready to sort and file the correspondence (step 4).**

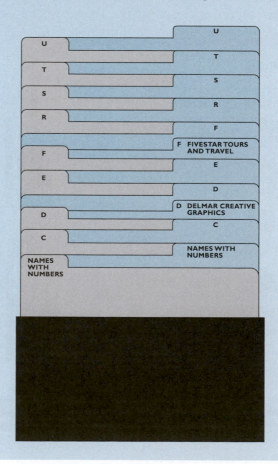

2. Remove correspondence pieces 16–30 and the cross-reference sheet from the forms pad.

3. For pieces 16–30, follow the Inspecting, Indexing, Cross-Referencing, and Coding steps on pages 34–39. Refer to the filing procedures on page 40 for pieces 16, 20, 23, 28, and 30. Cross-reference one record, piece 30. To review the procedure for cross-referencing alternative names, see Chapter 2, pages 17–18.

4. When all 15 pieces have been coded and cross-referenced, follow the Sorting and Filing steps on pages 39–41. Prepare the two new individual folders and file each folder behind its corresponding alphabetic guide. Merge pieces 16–30 with those already filed in Practical Application 3A.

5. Complete Checksheet 3B and give it to your instructor for checking. If you made any mistakes in filing, correct them before beginning Retrieval Exercise 3B.

6. Complete Retrieval Exercise 3B.

7. Keep your file box as it is; you will be using it in Practical Application 3C to interfile additional records.

- **Microfiche.** *Microfiche* is French, meaning "small card." Microfiche contain miniature images of records that appear in a gridlike pattern on 4-inch or 6-inch sheets of film. As many as several hundred pages may be printed on one microfiche, so a microfiche reader must be used to magnify the small print to reading size. Microfiche are filed according to an eye-legible caption or number at the top. Many offices and libraries have a special file where microfiche are filed by alphabet, subject, or number.

Indexing Records for Key Words

So far, you have indexed correspondence and forms by selecting the name under which to file each record. An additional type of indexing, called **key word indexing,** is used to locate records stored in computer word processing files or database files and in libraries that have card files. Although key word indexing is sometimes an automatic feature of records management software, many software programs require that the key words be selected and keyed by the software user. If a business uses a computer scanner to enter the records into a computer file, the records manager may index the key words manually or the scanning software may index the key words automatically.

To index for key words, the records manager must read each record and look for words in the text that capture its subject or content. A key word can also be a name or another proper noun. Usually, no more than five key words are used, with the average number being two or three. The key words can be used to search through a computer index or through a library card file when looking for records under a specific topic.

For example, for correspondence piece 1, which was indexed and filed under the name *Five-Star Tours and Travel*, these key words can be indexed:

1. BICYCLE
2. TOURS

Piece 28 was indexed under the name of the applicant, *Miss Socorro A. Ramirez*. Two key words can be indexed:

1. **RESUME**
2. **ACCOUNTING**

In Practical Application 3C, in addition to following the Inspecting, Indexing, Cross-Referencing, Coding, Sorting, and Filing steps, you will also index two key words for each of the new pieces 31–40. To assist you, a list of key words from which you can match two key words for each record is provided on Checksheet 3C, Part 1.

Follow these steps when indexing a record for key words in Practical Application 3C:

1. **Read the contents of the record.**

2. **Circle two words in the record that are relevant to the content.**

3. **Match the two key words you have selected with those in the list of key words.**

4. **Check key words in the list that have been selected; use each key word only once.**

5. **Print the two key words at the top of the record in the upper right corner.**

PRACTICAL APPLICATION 3C
Alphabetic Correspondence Filing and
Indexing Correspondence for Key Words   Time Goal: 1 Hour

Supplies   File box containing pieces 1–30 and cross-reference already filed
Correspondence pieces 31–40 (Forms Pad 4)
1 cross-reference sheet (Forms Pad 4)
Checksheet 3C Part 1 and Checksheet 3C Part 2
(Checksheet Packet)

Directions
Follow step-by-step.

1. **Remove correspondence pieces 31–40 and the cross-reference sheet from the forms pad.**

2. **For pieces 31–40, follow the Inspecting, Indexing, Cross-Referencing, and Coding steps on pages 34–39.**

3. **To index each piece for two key words, follow Steps 1–5 listed previously. Refer to the key words list provided in Part 1 of Checksheet 3C; write your selection of two key words for each of pieces 31–40 in the spaces provided.**

4. **When all 10 pieces have been coded, cross-referenced, and indexed for key words, sort and file them with those already filed in Practical Applications 3A and 3B.**

5. **Complete Checksheet 3C, Part 2, and give both parts of Checksheet 3C to your instructor for checking. If you made any mistakes, correct them before beginning the next Practical Application.**

6. **Keep your file box and files assembled.**

Handling Requests to Charge Out Records and Follow Up

People in various departments of The Learning Zone may want to **charge out** (borrow) records from your files. When processing a request to charge out records, you need to gather the following information:

- **WHAT record is being charged out?**
- **WHO is charging out the record?**
- **WHEN is the record being charged out?**
- **WHEN is the record going to be returned?**

Proceed as follows:

1. **The person borrowing a record fills in an OUT Sheet like the one shown in Figure 3-6. Complete any missing information on the OUT Sheet. If a person phones in a request, you must prepare the OUT Sheet. You allow a record to be borrowed for seven days.**

2. **Retrieve the record from the file.**

3. **Keep a record of the transaction by copying the information from the OUT Sheet onto a Charge-Out and Follow-Up Log, as shown in Figure 3-7.**

OUT

To: **Records Center**

Name of Record **Del Mar Creative Graphics**
Address **9330 Melrose Avenue**
Del Mar, CA   92014-1650

Date of Record **July 7, ----**
Subject **Invitations for August 28 Software Demonstration Workshop**
Date Borrowed **July 9, ----**

Requested By

Name **Mike Stavros**
Department **Marketing**
Date Due **July 16, ----**

Record No. **12**

FIGURE 3-6
OUT Sheet

CHARGE-OUT AND FOLLOW-UP LOG

OUT Sheet No.	Record No.	Name and Address of Record	Date of Record	Borrower	Date Borrowed	Date Due	Date Returned
Example	12	Del Mar Creative Graphics 9330 Melrose Avenue Del Mar, CA 92014-1650	7/7/--	Mike Stavros	7/9/--	7/16	

FIGURE 3-7
Charge-Out and Follow-Up Log

4. Place the OUT Sheet in the file as a substitute for the borrowed record. Keep the OUT Sheet in the file until the record is returned.

5. When the record is returned, record the date of return on the Charge-Out and Follow-Up Log, remove the OUT Sheet from the file, and place the returned record in the file.

PRACTICAL APPLICATION 3D
Handling Requests to Charge Out Records and Follow Up

Time Goal: 1 Hour

Supplies   File box containing pieces 1–40 and cross-references already filed
5 OUT Sheets, Nos. 1–5 (Forms Pad 4)
Checksheet 3D, Charge-Out and Follow-Up Log
(Checksheet Packet)

Directions
Follow step-by-step.
The following events take place over a two-week period in the records center at the Learning Zone. Follow the procedures explained on pages 49–50 for charging out records. The time goal for processing each OUT Sheet and recording the information on the Charge-Out and Follow-Up Log is 5 minutes. The *Name and Address of Record* column has already been filled in for you.

December 1, ----, Judy Harloff, Ph.D., Recycling Projects Director, sends in OUT Sheet 1. She wants the faxed letter of June 25 from Dartt University. Be sure to fill in the OUT Sheet with the due date (seven calendar days) and the record number of the Dartt University fax.

December 2, ----, The bookkeeper, Terri C. Limon, phones in a request for the letter to The Friendly Fitness Club of Marina del Rey. She is not sure of the date of the letter. Complete OUT Sheet 2.

December 5 ----, Delores Jackson, Editor of *Conservation Magazine,* sends in OUT Sheet 3.

December 8, ----, Judy Harloff returns the faxed letter from Dartt University. Record the date returned on the Charge-Out and Follow-Up Log for OUT Sheet 1, pull the OUT Sheet from the file, and replace it with the faxed letter. Save the OUT Sheet for checking by your instructor.

December 8, ----, Budget Director C. J. Trujillo e-mails a request for the spreadsheet dated September 30 prepared by United Stocks and Investments, Inc..

December 9, ----, Terri C. Limon returns the letter to The Friendly Fitness Club. Follow the necessary procedures. Save the OUT Sheet for checking by your instructor.

December 10, ----, Delores Jackson returns the letter from Caldano & de la Cruz, Attorneys-At-Law. Follow the necessary procedures. Save the OUT Sheet for checking by your instructor.

December 12, ----, Aiko Hata, Ph.D., Day-Care Center Director, sends in OUT Sheet 5 for the letter from the St. Francis Health Spa dated sometime in September.

Check your Charge-Out and Follow-Up Log to be sure it is up to date. Give it to your instructor for checking, along with the OUT Sheets for records that have been returned.

If your work is satisfactory, remove all items from the file box. Store the guides and folders in the appropriate envelopes and rearranges pieces 1–40 in numeric order. Discard the cross-reference sheets and OUT Sheets.

COMPUTER APPLICATION 3A (SEE APPENDIX A.)
Opening and Defining a Table, Adding Records, and Printing a Report

COMPUTER APPLICATION 3B (SEE APPENDIX A.)
Adding and Finding Records, Sorting Alphabetically, and Printing a Report

COMPUTER APPLICATION 3C (SEE APPENDIX A.)
Searching for Data

COMPUTER APPLICATION 3D (SEE APPENDIX A.)
Modifying Records, Deleting Records, Sorting, and Printing

Color-Coding Alphabetic Files

Color-coded folder labels are especially useful for files stored in vertical drawer file cabinets or on shelves because it takes less time to find and file a color-coded folder. When folders remain visible, as in an open-shelf system, using color on file folder labels helps the records manager identify misfiles because he or she can easily spot a color that is out of place.

There are several methods of color-coding. In this section, you will work with one method and will assign colors to names on folders in the Check Your Understanding exercise.

One method of color-coding is to divide the alphabet into five sections and to assign a different color to each section as follows:

ABCDE:	RED
FGHIJ:	BLUE
KLMNO:	GREEN
PQRST:	ORANGE
UVWXYZ:	PURPLE

The first two letters of the last name or of the key indexing unit of a business name are color-coded as shown in the following examples:

EXAMPLES:		
Name	**Colors on File Folder Label**	
Frances T. <u>Wa</u>io	PURPLE	RED
<u>Mr</u>. Timothy Designer Shoes	GREEN	ORANGE
Mrs. Richard <u>Kim</u>	GREEN	BLUE
Crystal <u>Br</u>adley, M.D.	RED	ORANGE

CHECK YOUR UNDERSTANDING

Color-Coding Alphabetic Files

Time Goal: 3 Minutes

Directions: For each of the following names, assign color-coded labels, using the following alphabetic color system. First, code each name by underlining the key unit and numbering the subsequent units. Then color-code the first two letters of the key indexing unit by writing the two colors next to each name in the spaces provided. Indicate the alphabetic order of the 10 names by numbering them from 1 to 10 in the parentheses.

Color-Coding System:

ABCDE:	RED
FGHIJ:	BLUE
KLMNO:	GREEN
PQRST:	ORANGE
UVWXYZ:	PURPLE

Name	Colors on File Folder Label	
( ) Michael F. DiCapprio	_____	_____
( ) San Diego State University	_____	_____
( ) Mr. Simon O'Shane	_____	_____
( ) Trina Bullette	_____	_____
( ) Mountain-View School	_____	_____
( ) John Wayne Sr. High School	_____	_____
( ) Silver Springs YMCA	_____	_____
( ) Children's Book Club	_____	_____
( ) Hassana S. Rama, M.D.	_____	_____
( ) Ms. Val Westley	_____	_____

See page 131 for the correct answers.

End-of-Chapter Activity

Scenario: Your company has decided to investigate the pros and cons of eliminating paper records. Your supervisor asks you to look into the possibility of hiring an outside company to scan the paper records that currently exist throughout the organization.

Using the Internet, gather information about document imaging. Then do the following three tasks. Share your information with the class.

1. **List three URLS and the names of the companies that provide paper scanning and document-imaging services.**

2. **After reading the descriptions of the scanning and document-imaging services provided, choose one company and list in bulleted format the services it provides.**

3. **List any unfamiliar technical terms that you encounter. Include their definitions.**

Chapter 4: Numeric Filing Procedures

Learning Goals

- Recognize the four components of a consecutive numeric file.
- Perform the six steps involved in processing correspondence and other documents for numeric filing.
- File computer printouts in consecutive numeric order in binders.
- File computer output microfiche (COM) in terminal-digit order.
- Color-code records in both consecutive and terminal-digit numeric files.

Introduction

Numeric filing is a frequently used filing method that arranges records according to numbers, either consecutively (1, 2, 3, 4, and so on), as shown in Figure 4-1, or nonconsecutively (in groups, such as 003-49-1251). Most often found in larger offices, such as government offices, legal and medical offices, financial institutions, and insurance companies, numeric filing systems are usually color-coded for efficient identification of records. By using color-coding in their numeric filing systems, organizations can reduce the time it takes to file and retrieve records by nearly 50 percent.

Numeric filing offers several advantages. Numbers on file folder labels usually require less space than names, and without visible names on the labels, confidentiality of the files is protected. Less time is usually required to train personnel to use a numeric filing system. In fact, most people find it easier and faster to work with numbers. For example, if you were to ask a

FIGURE 4-1

Numeric Filing System

person to answer these two questions, his or her response to the first question would probably be much faster:

What number precedes 684?

What letter precedes X?

Consecutive filing, or **serial filing** as it is often called, is the numeric filing method you will practice in Practical Application 4A. Numeric serial filing is often used to process invoices, sales orders, requisitions, and other office forms. Each record is numbered, and all records that follow are given a progressively higher number.

Nonconsecutive numbering methods use groups of two, three, or four digits when numbers are assigned to records, as in social security numbers or telephone numbers. In nonconsecutive filing, new records are distributed evenly throughout the files. You will use terminal-digit filing, a nonconsecutive numbering method, in Practical Application 4B. In terminal-digit numeric filing, the last group of numbers is the key indexing unit.

Consecutive Numeric Filing

Four components make up a consecutive numeric file:

1. **Serially Numbered Folders with Guides.** Correspondence is filed in folders that have numbered tabs. (Some offices include both the correspondent's name and number on the folder tab.) Folders are filed in consecutive numeric order, with the lowest numbers first. Numeric guides divide the drawer or shelf between every 5 or 10 folders to facilitate the filing and retrieving of records.

2. **General Alphabetic Folders and Guides.** An alphabetic section behind a guide labeled *GENERAL* is reserved for those records that have not yet been assigned numbers. A record is filed in the general alphabetic section of the numeric file according to the correspondent's name if it is only the first (or second) item for a correspondent. When there is a second (or third) record regarding the same correspondent, a number is assigned, a numbered folder is prepared, and the numeric folder containing the records is filed in the numeric section.

   The general alphabetic section may be placed in front of or behind the numeric section. The most logical placement is in front because the consecutive numeric file expands at the back of the file.

3. **Alphabetic Index.** The alphabetic index may be in the form of a list (see Figure 4-2 on the next page) or a card file (see Figure 4-3 on the next page). The alphabetic index shows the number assigned to each correspondent and indicates cross-referenced names. Cross-referencing names in the alphabetic index eliminates the need to prepare cross-reference sheets for the correspondence file. If the index is on cards, each card shows the name, address, and file number of one correspondent.

   The alphabetic index is the first place you check when you file or retrieve records from a numeric file. The list or cards show the number assigned to each correspondent or show a *G* to indicate that the correspondence is located in the general alphabetic section. Names that are cross-referenced show either a *GX* or a number and an *X*. Accuracy of this index is essential to the efficient operation of the numeric filing method.

4. **Accession Log.** The accession log, sometimes called an **accession record or book,** is used to keep a record of the numbers that have been

FIGURE 4-2
Alphabetic Index List

ALPHABETIC INDEX	
Name	**File No.**
AARONS GERALD S	G
BUSTAMONTE AND INGLES	G
CALDWELL JESSICA SKYE	G
COLEMAN AND WILLIAMS INC	503X
CULVER CITY ANIMAL HOSPITAL	G
GREENBERG MELANIA DDS	G
GREWAL SUKI L	501
HANS GRAPHIC DESIGN	502
HARRINGTON WILLIAM GENE	G
INGLES AND BUSTAMONTE	GX
MYRA SIEGAL ASSOCIATES	500
OBRIANS SURF SHOP	G
ROSE CAFE	G
WILLIAMS AND COLEMAN INC	503

FIGURE 4-3
Alphabetic Index
Cards

Original Card

WILLIAMS AND COLEMAN INC	503

2   3   4
Williams & Coleman, Inc.
7331 Venice Boulevard
Los Angeles, CA 90023-0021

Cross-Reference Card

COLEMAN AND WILLIAMS INC	503X

SEE: WILLIAMS AND COLEMAN INC

assigned and to show the next available number. After you check the alphabetic index and determine that a correspondent does not already have a number, write the name of the correspondent in the accession log on the next available line. An example of an accession log is shown in Figure 4-4.

FIGURE 4-4
Accession Log

ACCESSION LOG		
File No.	**Name of Correspondent**	**Date Assigned**
500	MYRA SIEGAL ASSOCIATES	10/03
501	GREWAL SUKI L	10/04
502	HANS GRAPHIC DESIGN	10/04
503	WILLIAMS AND COLEMAN INC	10/15
504		
505		

and so on

Numeric Filing Procedures

Step 1: Inspecting

Make sure the records are ready to be filed. On incoming correspondence or forms, look for release marks, such as initials or the word *FILE* or *PAID*. Copies of outgoing correspondence do not need release marks.

Step 2: Indexing and Coding

Determine the name under which the record should be filed. If necessary, review the rules in Chapter 3 for indexing correspondence. Code the key unit in the name by underlining it and number the subsequent units.

If the name is to be cross-referenced, code it in cross-reference form as explained in Chapter 3, pages 37–38. Remember, in numeric filing, cross-referencing is done in the alphabetic index only. Review the format for a cross-reference card for a numeric card file in Figure 4-2.

Step 3: Sorting

When working with many records, sort the records in alphabetic order according to the key unit of each piece *before* checking the alphabetic index.

Step 4: Number Assignment

For each piece, check the alphabetic index to determine whether the name is listed. If it is, either a number or a G (for *general*) will appear.

1. **If the name has been assigned a number.** Write the number in the upper right corner of the record. File the record in the corresponding numeric folder, placing the most recently dated record in front.

2. **If the name has been assigned a G.** The correspondence is filed in the general alphabetic section. File the record in the appropriate general folder. Records within each general folder are filed alphabetically by correspondent name.

   In Practical Application 4A, a correspondent is assigned a number when two or more pieces have accumulated. To assign a number, check the accession log to find the next available number and write the correspondent's name in indexing order on the line next to the number. Write this number on all of the correspondent's records. Also be sure to change the *G* in the alphabetic index by drawing a line through it and writing the newly assigned number: ̶G352.

   Prepare a new numeric folder and put all of the correspondent's records inside with the most recent in front. Place the folder in the correct sequence in the numeric file.

3. **If the name is not listed in the index.** The record must be for a new correspondent, assuming that the alphabetic index is accurate and that you checked thoroughly. Add the new name to the alphabetic index and assign a *G* code. If you are working with a card file, prepare a new card that includes the correspondent's name and address and a *G*. Write a *G* on the record in the upper right corner and file the record in the general alphabetic section.

Step 5: Numeric Sorting

If you are working with many records at one time (10 or more), you can save time by sorting the records into numeric groups of 10s, 100s, or 1,000s before filing.

Step 6: Filing and Retrieval

For records regarding the same correspondent, remember that the most recently dated correspondence is filed in front. Records within general folders are filed alphabetically by correspondent name. Each record should take only about 15 seconds to file.

When retrieving records from a numeric file, always check the alphabetic index first to determine the file number or G code. Charge-out and follow-up procedures are the same as for alphabetic filing. Be sure to replace a borrowed record with an OUT Sheet, a requisition slip, a charge-out card, or another similar form that shows the date borrowed, the name of the person who borrowed the record, the subject of the record, and the due date. No OUT Sheets are needed in Practical Application 4A.

PRACTICAL APPLICATION 4A
Consecutive Numeric Correspondence
and Forms Filing
Time Goal: 1½ Hours

Supplies File box
Correspondence and forms pieces 1–40, previously used, arranged in order from 1 to 40
2 unprinted guides (Envelope 1)
2 yellow guide labels: GENERAL and 650 (Envelope 1)
9 previously used general alphabetic preprinted folders: NAMES WITH NUMBERS, C, D, E, F, R, S, T, U
6 new unprinted folders (Envelope 3) and 4 previously used folders
10 yellow folder labels: 650, 651, 652, 653, 654, 655, 656, 657, 658, 659 (Envelope 1)
Checksheet 4A (Checksheet Packet):
Alphabetic Index
Accession Log
General Alphabetic File
Numeric Correspondence File
Retrieval Exercise 4A (Checksheet Packet)

Directions
Follow step-by-step.

1. Attach the 2 yellow guide labels to the guides and the 10 yellow folder labels to the folders.
2. Set up the GENERAL guide and general alphabetic folders as shown in the following illustration. Place the numeric guide, 650, behind the general folders.
3. Keep the 10 numeric folders (labeled 650–659) in a separate pile until they are assigned to correspondents.

4. Work first with pieces 1–20. Follow Steps 1–6, pages 57–58. Because you coded those pieces in previous Practical Applications, you do not need to repeat that step. The alphabetic index for this application is a list rather than a card file; therefore, you do not need to prepare cross-reference cards.

   Remember to sort the pieces alphabetically before checking the alphabetic index (Checksheet 4A). For your convenience, names have been provided in the alphabetic index on Checksheet 4A. (**Note:** Although the names are already listed, no records have yet been processed for the correspondents.) Assign a *G* to the first record for a correspondent. Write a *G* in the blank provided on the alphabetic index and in the upper right corner of the record.

   When a second record for the same correspondent is received, write the name of the correspondent in indexing order on the next blank line in the accession log (Checksheet 4A). Cross out the *G* beside the correspondent's name in the alphabetic index and write the assigned number beside it. Write the number on all records for that correspondent.

5. After you have processed and filed pieces 1–20, repeat the numeric filing steps for pieces 21–40. Instructions for piece 30: Assign numeric folder 659 to TURNER TYLER. Place the letter from his mother, STFRANCIS DEANA MARIE (piece 18), in the numeric folder with piece 30. Write 659X next to STFRANCIS DEANA MARIE in the alphabetic index to indicate where the correspondence can be found.

6. When pieces 21–40 have been processed and filed, record the contents of the numeric correspondence file and the general alphabetic file on Checksheet 4A. Give both pages of Checksheet 4A to your instructor for checking. If you made any mistakes in filing, correct them before beginning Retrieval Exercise 4A.

7. Complete Retrieval Exercise 4A.

8. When you have completed Retrieval Exercise 4A and your work has been approved, remove correspondence pieces 1–40 from the file and rearrange them in numeric sequence.

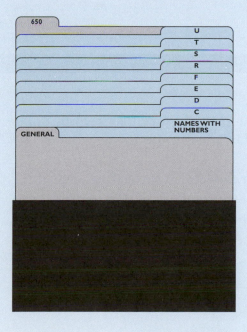

9. **Remove all guides and folders from the file box and store them in the appropriate envelopes.**

COMPUTER APPLICATION 4A (SEE APPENDIX A.)
Adding Records, Adding a Field, Numeric Sorting, and Printing

Filing Records in Binders

Oversized records require a different method of storage. For example, computer-generated output may be on large sheets of paper called **computer printouts.** Because these printouts are usually large and bulky, they may be filed in binders (see Figure 4-5) and kept on shelves or hung from racks. Magazines, maps, and other oversized records may also be filed in binders.

FIGURE 4-5
Printouts in Binders

CHECK YOUR UNDERSTANDING

Filing Printouts in Numeric Binders   Time Goal: 3 Minutes

Directions: The five binders shown in the following illustration and list contain records of customer accounts for a large manufacturer. Each binder holds printouts arranged in consecutive order.

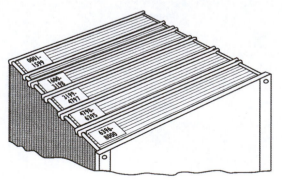

Binder 01: Account No. 0001 to 1599
Binder 02: Account No. 1600 to 3198
Binder 03: Account No. 3199 to 4797
Binder 04: Account No. 4798 to 6395
Binder 05: Account No. 6396 to 8000

Following are 10 account numbers. Next to each account number, write the number of the binder (from 01 to 05) that contains the printout for that account.

	Account No.	**Binder No.**
Example:	**3307**	03
1.	3107	
2.	6506	
3.	0008	
4.	1101	
5.	7999	
6.	4844	
7.	3691	
8.	4695	
9.	2748	
10.	5263	

See page 131 for the correct answers.

Terminal-Digit (Nonconsecutive) Numeric Filing

In the consecutive numeric filing method you used in Practical Application 4A, numeric folders 650–659 were added at the end of the file. The next folder to be added would have been 660. In such a consecutive numeric file, the numbers assigned grow larger and expansion of the file occurs at the end. The large numbers may cause misfiling, and the process of adding new folders only to the end of the file may result in inefficient filing and retrieval of records.

Terminal-digit numeric filing was developed to make numeric filing and retrieval more efficient. Numbers are assigned to correspondents in groups of two or three digits. Reading from right to left, the last (or terminal) digits are the key indexing units. For example, 12-43-89 is read as 89, 43, and then 12.

12	43	89
(third unit or final number)	(second unit or secondary number)	(key unit or primary number)

In the following example, the numbers at the left are listed in consecutive numeric filing order. On the right, the same numbers are listed in terminal-digit filing order.

Consecutive Order	Terminal-Digit Order
19-83-52	45-92-18
23-61-48	23-61-48
23-72-81	39-72-51
39-14-51	19-83-52
45-92-18	47-83-52
47-83-52	23-72-81

In the terminal-digit numeric filing method, the key indexing unit is the last (or terminal) group of numbers. If the key indexing units are the same, second units are compared, and so on.

The groups of digits usually represent the location of the folder in a storage container. As illustrated in Figure 4-6, the primary number often corresponds to a numbered file drawer, the secondary number corresponds to a number guide, and the third or final number corresponds to the folder number.

Before completing Practical Application 4B, you will practice arranging one type of microimage media, COM (computer output microfilm or microfiche), in terminal-digit order.

Instead of printing information on bulky sheets of printout paper, the computer can produce microfiche. The microimages are many times smaller

FIGURE 4-6

Terminal-Digit Order

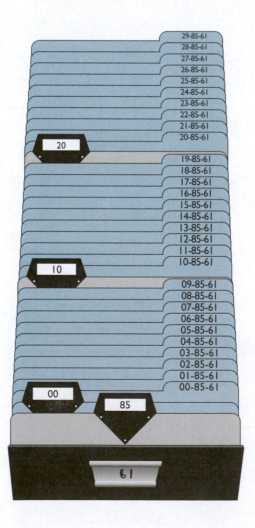

than ordinary microfiche, with 4,000 or more pages on one 4-inch × 6-inch COM. The computer can also produce COM in digital form, so the information can be transferred electronically.

CHECK YOUR UNDERSTANDING

Terminal-Digit Numeric Filing

Time Goal: 2 Minutes

Directions: Arrange the 10 COM in terminal-digit order by numbering them from 1 to 10 in the parentheses provided.

Examples: 047-01-822 (2)
012-33-641 (1)
045-06-822 (3)

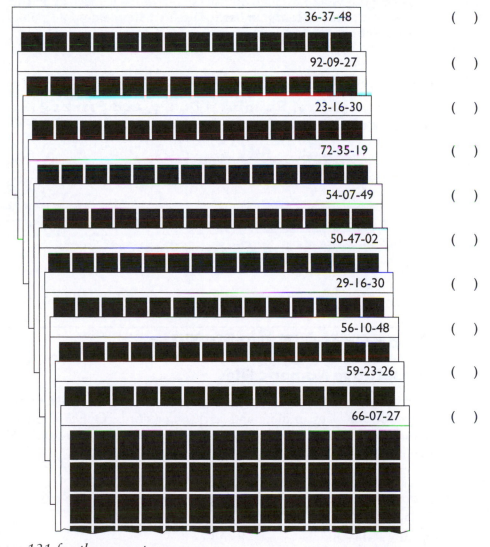

36-37-48 ( )

92-09-27 ( )

23-16-30 ( )

72-35-19 ( )

54-07-49 ( )

50-47-02 ( )

29-16-30 ( )

56-10-48 ( )

59-23-26 ( )

66-07-27 ( )

See page 131 for the correct answers.

PRACTICAL APPLICATION 4B
Arranging Cards in Terminal-Digit Order   Time Goal: 10 Minutes

Supplies Cards 1–25, previously used in Chapter 2, arranged in numeric order from 1 to 25 Checksheet 4B (Checksheet Packet)

Directions
Follow step-by-step.

1. Using cards 1–25 from Chapter 2, arrange the 25 cards in order according to the terminal-digit numeric method. To do so, first sort the cards by the terminal digits. Then sort those cards having the same terminal digits (key units) by the second units. A third sort by the final units may be needed.

2. On Checksheet 4B, record the card numbers and the terminal-digit numbers of the cards arranged in terminal-digit order. Give Checksheet 4B to your instructor for checking.

3. After your work has been approved, rearrange cards 1–25 in consecutive numeric order by card number for use in a Supplemental Computer Application.

COMPUTER APPLICATION 4B (SEE APPENDIX A.)
Creating a Query, Running a Query, and Printing the Results of a Query

Color-Coding Numeric Files

Consecutive Numeric Files

As with alphabetic files, color-coded labels on numeric folders help to improve the efficiency of filing and retrieving records. One type of consecutive numeric color-coding system assigns color codes to the first two digits of a file number as follows:

0:	RED	5:	BROWN
1:	ORANGE	6:	LIGHT GREEN
2:	PINK	7:	DARK BLUE
3:	LIGHT BLUE	8:	YELLOW
4:	PURPLE	9:	DARK GREEN

EXAMPLES:

File No.	Colors on File Folder Label	
5481	BROWN	PURPLE
9730	DARK GREEN	DARK BLUE
2816	PINK	YELLOW
3103	LIGHT BLUE	ORANGE
4419	PURPLE	PURPLE

CHECK YOUR UNDERSTANDING

Color-Coding Consecutive Numeric Files

Time Goal: 2 Minutes

Directions: For each of the 10 file numbers, assign color-coded labels, using the numeric color-coding system shown in the previous section. Color-code the first two digits of each file number. Then arrange the file numbers in consecutive numeric order by numbering them from 1 to 10 in the parentheses provided.

File No.	Colors on File Folder Label	
( ) 68130	_____	_____
( ) 20739	_____	_____
( ) 24295	_____	_____
( ) 31968	_____	_____
( ) 57291	_____	_____
( ) 07313	_____	_____
( ) 43411	_____	_____
( ) 86105	_____	_____
( ) 01630	_____	_____
( ) 19055	_____	_____

See page 132 for the correct answers.

Terminal-Digit Numeric Files

A terminal-digit numeric system is color-coded by the terminal digits. As in consecutive numeric filing, 10 separate colors may be used to represent digits 0 through 9.

0: RED	5: BROWN	
1: ORANGE	6: LIGHT GREEN	
2: PINK	7: DARK BLUE	
3: LIGHT BLUE	8: YELLOW	
4: PURPLE	9: DARK GREEN	

EXAMPLES:

File No.	Colors on File Folder Label	
507-81-36	LIGHT BLUE	LIGHT GREEN
467-26-08	RED	YELLOW
235-42-95	DARK GREEN	BROWN
871-25-23	PINK	LIGHT BLUE

CHECK YOUR UNDERSTANDING

Color-Coding Terminal-Digit Numeric Files

Time Goal: 2 Minutes

Directions: For each of the 10 file numbers, assign color-coded labels, using the numeric color-coding system in the previous section. Color-code the terminal digits of each file number. Then arrange the file numbers in terminal-digit order by numbering them from 1 to 10 in the parentheses provided.

File No.	Colors on File Folder Label	
( ) 534-40-94	_____	_____
( ) 407-66-26	_____	_____
( ) 021-17-79	_____	_____
( ) 180-59-51	_____	_____
( ) 357-62-23	_____	_____
( ) 292-62-94	_____	_____
( ) 375-18-79	_____	_____
( ) 219-34-50	_____	_____
( ) 935-38-44	_____	_____
( ) 599-62-94	_____	_____

See page 132 for the correct answers.

Bar-Coding Files

As technology advances, more efficient methods of managing files are being developed and used by records managers. Bar-coding file folders improves the accuracy of the filing, charge-out, and retrieval processes. Just as a store keeps track of its merchandise by scanning the UPC (Universal Product Code) of a customer's purchase, records managers can keep track of their files by scanning bar codes on file folder labels. The bar codes are read either by portable bar code readers, called wands, or by keyboard-attached bar code scanners. Records management software can automatically print bar-coded labels. Each folder is then identifiable by its unique bar code. An example of a bar-coded label and wand is shown in Figure 4-7.

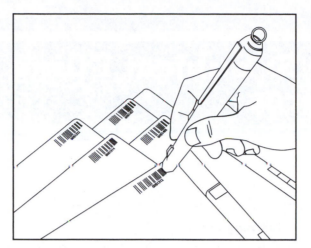

FIGURE 4-7
Bar-Coded Label and Wand

End-of-Chapter Activity

Learn more about microimage technology, such as microfilm and microfiche, to answer these questions:

1. **What are some of the advantages and disadvantages of using microimage technology for records storage and retrieval?**

2. **Based on what you've learned, what do you think the future of microimage technology will be?**

At your library or on the Internet, find at least two sources of information that you could recommend to the class. Include those sources in a one-page summary.

Chapter 5: Subject Filing Procedures

Learning Goals

- Follow the six steps involved in processing correspondence and other documents for subject filing.
- Arrange CD-ROMs in subject order.

Introduction

As more information flows throughout an organization, the importance of being able to locate and retrieve information when it is needed becomes critical. The information contained in records is a valuable resource that must be managed as effectively as other resources in the organization. In addition to working with correspondence, in this chapter, you will learn the best practices for managing the ever-increasing amount of e-mail.

Storing records solely by subject matter or topic instead of by the name of an individual, a business, or an organization, is known as **subject filing.** Subject filing should be used when other systems will not be effective or when documents cannot be filed by any other single filing characteristic. All correspondence has a specific subject, or theme. The records manager must read each piece of correspondence to determine its subject.

An **alphabetic subject index** lists all subject titles used in a subject filing system. A records manager should make sure that the subjects selected are clear and accurate. The subject titles in the alphabetic subject index should be recorded on cards and arranged alphabetically or should be kept in the form of an alphabetic list stored in a computer or on paper. Some subject indexes combine subjects and numbers by assigning a code number to each subject.

Cross-referencing is necessary when a piece of correspondence contains more than one subject. In subject filing, only subjects are cross-referenced. Cross-referencing can be done either by placing cross-reference sheets in the correspondence file or by listing the cross-references in the alphabetic subject index. In Practical Application 5, you will prepare cross-reference sheets for the correspondence file.

Subject Filing Procedures

Step 1: Inspecting

Check each record to make sure it has been released for filing. Release marks are explained in Chapter 3, pages 34–35.

Step 2: Indexing

Read each record carefully to determine what subject (or multiple subjects) it contains. Find the important theme that will most clearly identify the record for retrieval.

Your next task is to match the subject of the record with a subject title already in the alphabetic subject index. The subject titles listed in the alphabetic subject index are usually compiled by the records manager or by someone else in the company who has experience and knowledge of the types of subject titles required.

If information about more than one subject is included in the piece of correspondence, decide what the cross-reference will be. The cross-referenced subject title should also be selected from the alphabetic subject index.

Within each subject folder, correspondence is arranged alphabetically according to the names of the correspondents. Therefore, as part of the indexing step for each piece, you should also index the name of the correspondent. For a memorandum, the name of the correspondent is the writer of the memo—the name after *FROM*. The procedures for indexing the name of the correspondent on incoming and outgoing correspondence are described in Chapter 3, pages 36–37.

Following are the necessary indexing steps:

1. **Read each piece to determine the subject.**
2. **Match the subject with one listed in the alphabetic subject index.**
3. **If more than one subject is included in the document, decide what the cross-referenced subject will be.**
4. **Index the name of the correspondent.**

In Practical Application 5, you will work with 25 pieces of correspondence. The first 15 pieces to be indexed were used in previous Practical Applications (pieces 26–40). You have already indexed the correspondents' names for these pieces; therefore, your task will be to select the subject of each piece. All four indexing steps listed previously will be necessary for the remaining 10 pieces (pieces 41–50) of new correspondence.

Step 3: Coding

When subject titles contain more than one word, writing all of the words on the records is very time-consuming. Subject coding is made easier by using three-letter subject codes. Subject codes may be comprised of the first letter of each word in the subject title. For example, COMPUTER SOFTWARE DEVELOPMENT may be coded as CSD. If only one word appears in the subject title, the three-letter code may be the first letter of the word and the next two consonants in the word; for example, ADM may be used for ADMINISTRATION. Any two other consonants that give a clear indication of the subject title are acceptable also, as in using MGT for MANAGEMENT.

Subject titles or codes are written on the piece of correspondence in the upper right corner.

A subject title to be cross-referenced is underlined with a wavy line, and an *X* is placed in the right margin. If subject codes are used, the code for the cross-referenced subject may be written above the *X*. (See Figure 5-1.)

Also remember to code the correspondent's name according to the alphabetic indexing rules in Chapter 2.

Step 4: Cross-Referencing

Prepare a cross-reference sheet for the file when more than one subject is included in a record. At the top of the cross-reference sheet, write the second subject title. The second subject must also be selected from those listed in the alphabetic subject index.

FIGURE 5-1

Subject-Coded
Correspondence

PIR

November 16, ----

Mrs. Claudia Tremaine
R. J. DeVille Mfg.
122 S.W. 11th Street
Sacramento, CA 95813-6002

Dear Mrs. Tremaine:

Thank you for your request for information about ways in which R. J. DeVille Mfg. can help to preserve the protective layer of ozone in Earth's upper atmosphere. We are happy to provide this public information service.

Your company can indeed help by reducing its emissions of chemicals. As part *PCP* of your conservation project, strive for complete phaseout of production and X use of harmful chemicals as soon as possible. As explained in the enclosed report, there are nonpolluting substitutes for many harmful chemicals. The report also contains a list of practical alternatives already in use throughout the world.

If you would like one of our consultants to meet with you to help plan your conservation project, we would be pleased to arrange it.

Sincerely,

Eduardo Granados

Eduardo Granados
Director, Worldwide Conservation Projects

bv

Enclosure

35

In the space provided after the SEE notation, indicate the original subject under which the record is filed.

SEE _original subject_ _____

File the record under the original subject. File the cross-reference sheet under the second subject.

Look at the Alphabetic Subject Index for Practical Application 5 on page 77. Those are the subjects used by The Learning Zone for its subject file.

Let's use correspondence piece 35, shown in Figure 5-1, as an example. This is one of the pieces you will file in Practical Application 5. After reading piece 35, a letter to R. J. DeVille Mfg., you should realize that it answers Mrs. Tremaine's request for public information and should be filed under this subject:

PROGRAMS

INFORMATION REQUESTS (subject title selected from the alphabetic subject index for Practical Application 5, page 77)

Code: PIR

The name of the correspondent is coded in the inside address: R. J. DeVille Mfg.

Because the letter also mentions that R. J. DeVille Mfg. is planning a conservation project to help protect the environment, you should prepare a cross-reference under this second subject:

PROGRAMS

CONSERVATION PROJECTS (subject title selected from the Alphabetic Subject Index for Practical Application 5)

Code: PCP

Remember to place a wavy line under the cross-referenced subject on the piece of correspondence. Also place an X and the subject code in the right margin. Your correspondence piece and cross-reference sheet should look like the ones shown in Figures 5-1 and 5-2, respectively.

Step 5: Sorting

Sort records alphabetically according to their main subject heading.

Example: **Computer Software**

     F̲inance

     P̲rograms

Place all records with the same main subject together. If records contain subheadings, as they do in Practical Application 5, sort the records first by the main heading and then by the subheading.

Example: **FIT**

     PE̲R

     LE̲D

     PL̲A

Step 6: Filing and Retrieval

In each subject folder, arrange the records alphabetically according to the names of the correspondents. If you have two or more pieces pertaining to

FIGURE 5-2
Cross-Reference Sheet

CROSS-REFERENCE SHEET

Name or Subject PCP

Address R. J. DeVille Mfg.

     122 S.W. 11th Street

     Sacramento, CA 95813-6002

Date of Record November 16, ----

Brief Summary Conservation of the ozone layer

SEE PIR

    R. J. Deville Mfg.

Your Name
———————————————
Records Manager

Current Date
———————————————
Date

35X
———————————————
Cross-Reference No.

the same correspondent, arrange the pieces according to the date, with the most recent date in front.

Procedures for processing requests to charge out records are the same as those for alphabetic and numeric filing; however, when completing an OUT Sheet in subject filing, write the subject title on the *Name of Record* line. No OUT Sheets are needed in Practical Application 5.

✓ CHECK YOUR UNDERSTANDING

Subject Filing Procedures   Time Goal: 5 Minutes

Directions: An alphabetic subject index and two pieces of correspondence (A and B) are shown next. Follow the Inspecting, Indexing, Coding, and Cross-Referencing steps to prepare these pieces for filing. (You do not need to actually prepare the cross-reference sheet.) Then answer the questions following each piece of correspondence.

Alphabetic Subject Index

ADVERTISING
- BOOKS—**ABK**
- INTERNET—**AIN**
- MAGAZINES—**AMG**
- NEWSPAPERS—**ANW**

APPLICATIONS
- ADMINISTRATIVE ASSISTANT—**AAA**
- EXECUTIVE SECRETARY—**AES**
- RECORDS MANAGER—**ARM**
- WORD PROCESSING SPECIALIST—**AWP**

FINANCE
- ACCOUNTS PAYABLE—**FAP**
- ACCOUNTS RECEIVABLE—**FAR**
- INCOME TAXES—**FIT**

MARKETING
- DISTRIBUTION—**MDS**
- SALES CAMPAIGNS—**MSC**
- SURVEYS—**MSR**

Correspondence Piece A

February 20, ----

Ms. Rebecca Shi
3740 Moorestown Drive
Tampa, FL 33601-4400

Dear Ms. Shi:

You successfully passed the employment exams and had an outstanding interview for the position of records manager. We are writing to let you know that your application for employment with the Tampa City Mayor's Office has been approved.

New-employee orientation will be held on Monday, March 8, in the Personnel Division at 9 a.m. We are looking forward to seeing you then.

Sincerely

Monica Ingle
Director of Human Resources

lm

Questions about Correspondence Piece A

1. Has piece A been released for filing?_____ How do you know? _____

_____

2. What is the subject of the letter? _____

_____

3. What is the name of the correspondent in indexing order? _____

_____

4. Describe the way you coded the subject and the name of the correspondent. _____

_____

5. What will be the arrangement of the records in the subject folder? _____

_____

6. Is there a need for a cross-reference? _____ If yes, under what subject? _____

_____

Correspondence
Piece B

**A-1
ADVERTISING
AGENCY**

18 East 54th Street • Washington • DC • 20001-2004 1-202-555-0177
http://www.a1adagency.com

April 18, ----

APR 20, ----, 11:10

Websphere Technologies, Inc.
30 West Hampton Avenue
Suite 488
Boston, MA 02106-3400

Ladies and Gentlemen:

You have an outstanding line of cutting-edge technology products and
services. To help increase your client base in the United States and abroad,
you could benefit from more worldwide exposure. Let the experts at A-1
Advertising plan an Internet multimedia advertising campaign for your
company.

A-1 Advertising Agency has the marketing experience and expertise to
design a sales campaign tailored to the special needs of your business. Give
us a call today!

Sincerely,

Arthur Monahan, Jr.

Arthur Monahan, Jr.
Internet Advertising Specialist
amonahan@a1adagency.com

inm

Questions about Correspondence Piece B

1. Has piece B been released for filing? _____ How do you know? _____

    _____

2. What is the subject of the letter? _____

3. What is the name of the correspondent in indexing order? _____

    _____

4. Describe the way you coded the subject and the name of the correspondent. _____

    _____

5. What will be the arrangement of the records in the subject folder? _____

    _____

6. Is there a need for a cross-reference? _____ If yes, under what subject? _____

    _____

See page 132 for the correct answers.

CHECK YOUR UNDERSTANDING

Arranging CD-ROMs in Subject Order

Time Goal: 2 Minutes

Directions: Arrange these 10 CD-ROMs in alphabetical order according to their subject captions by numbering them from 1 to 10 in the parentheses provided.

( ) BOOKS—SPEED SPANISH

( ) MUSIC—TCHAIKOVSKY - NUTCRACKER

( ) GAMES—BASEBALL PRO

( ) SOFTWARE—PHOTO FIXER

( ) MUSIC—TCHAIKOVSKY - SWAN LAKE

( ) GAMES—WORD CHALLENGE

( ) BOOKS—MANAGEMENT MADE EASY

( ) BOOKS—MONEY MANAGEMENT

( ) SOFTWARE—GRAPHICS DESIGNER

( ) MUSIC—BEETHOVEN PIANO CONCERTOS

CD-ROM Storage

CD-ROMs

See page 133 for the correct answers.

WORKPLACE FOCUS

Managing E-mail

In 2006, the number of e-mail messages sent daily is expected to exceed 60 billion worldwide, up from 31 billion in 2002.[1] The flow of e-mail in and out of an organization presents a huge challenge because e-mail correspondence and attachments are records that need to be managed as carefully as paper correspondence, digital files, and microimage records. Compounding the challenge is the fact that e-mail messages can be used as evidence in a lawsuit or regulatory investigation. Every organization needs to establish rules and policies for managing e-mail. Employees require training to determine what incoming and outgoing e-mail needs to be saved, where it should be stored (on the hard drive or on the network), and how long it must be retained.

Determining whether e-mail is an actual record depends on its content and the context of the message and attachments. Consider the following two points when making the determination:

- **Does the e-mail message involve business transactions that have occurred or are being planned?**

- **Does the e-mail message document discussion or decisions that have been made in relation to the business transaction?**

ARMA International has published a standard set of guidelines that are useful to organizations developing policies for managing e-mail, "Requirements for Managing Electronic Messages as Records."[2] Among the guidelines are statements that should be included in an organization's e-mail policy; for example:

- **The electronic message system and contents belong to the organization.**

- **The content of electronic messages qualifies as recorded information.**

- **Specific procedures are followed for handling records during litigation.**

- **The organization or employer retains rights for monitoring.**

With more than 60 billion electronic messages circulating daily throughout the world, your training in records management will help your organization establish and follow best practices in managing its e-mail.

[1] M. Levitt, *Email Usage Forecast and Analysis, 2000–2005.* International Data Corporation, IDC Report #23011, September 2000.

[2] ARMA International, *Requirements for Managing Electronic Messages as Records,* 2004.

PRACTICAL APPLICATION 5
Subject Filing

Time Goal: $1\frac{1}{2}$ Hours

Supplies	File box
	Correspondence pieces 26–40, previously used
	New correspondence pieces 41–50 (Forms Pad 4)
	3 previously used guides
	3 blue guide labels (Envelope 1): COMPUTER SOFTWARE
	FINANCE
	PROGRAMS

13 previously used folders
13 blue folder labels (Envelope 1):

CSD	COMPUTER SOFTWARE—DEVELOPMENT
CSM	COMPUTER SOFTWARE—MARKETING
CST	COMPUTER SOFTWARE—TESTING
FCR	FINANCE—CORPORATE RECORDS
FIT	FINANCE—INCOME TAX
FIV	FINANCE—INVOICES
FPR	FINANCE—PERSONNEL
PCP	PROGRAMS—CONSERVATION PROJECTS
PDC	PROGRAMS—DAY-CARE CENTER
PED	PROGRAMS—EDUCATION
PEP	PROGRAMS—ENVIRONMENTAL REQUESTS
PIR	PROGRAMS—INFORMATION REQUESTS
PLA	PROGRAMS—LEGISLATIVE ACTION

2 cross-reference sheets (Forms Pad 4)
Alphabetic Subject Index (provided here)
Checksheet 5 (Checksheet Packet)
Retrieval Exercise 5 (Checksheet Packet)

Directions

Follow step-by-step.

1. Attach the 3 blue guide labels to the guides and the 13 blue folder labels to the folders.

2. Set up the guides and folders as shown in the following illustration.

3. For each correspondence piece 26–50, follow the subject filing steps on pages 69–72. The alphabetic subject index follows this step. Prepare two cross-references, one for piece 35 and one for piece 45. The procedure for cross-referencing piece 35 is explained on pages 70–71.

4. After you have processed and filed the correspondence, complete Checksheet 5 and give it to your instructor for checking. If you made any mistakes in filing, correct them before beginning Retrieval Exercise 5.

5. Complete Retrieval Exercise 5.

ALPHABETIC SUBJECT INDEX

Subjects	Subject Codes	Subjects	Subject Codes
Computer Software		Programs	
Development	CSD	Conservation Projects	PCP
Marketing	CSM	Day-Care Center	PDC
Testing	CST	Education	PED
		Environmental Proposals	PEP
Finance		Information Requests	PIR
Corporate Records	FCR	Legislative Action	PLA
Income Tax	FIT		
Invoices	FIV		
Personnel	FPR		

6. When you have completed Retrieval Exercise 5 and your work has been approved, remove the correspondence pieces and rearrange them in numeric order with the others (1–50). Discard the cross-reference sheets.

7. Remove all guides and folders from the file box and store them in the appropriate envelopes.

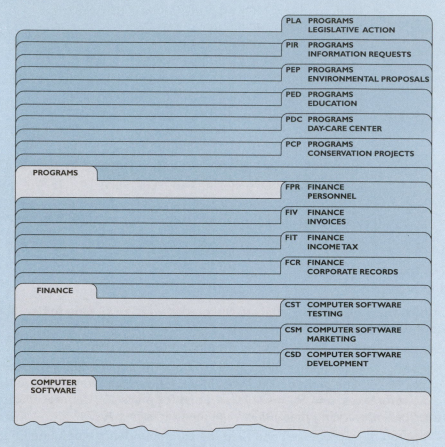

PLA PROGRAMS
     LEGISLATIVE ACTION

PIR PROGRAMS
     INFORMATION REQUESTS

PEP PROGRAMS
     ENVIRONMENTAL PROPOSALS

PED PROGRAMS
     EDUCATION

PDC PROGRAMS
     DAY-CARE CENTER

PCP PROGRAMS
     CONSERVATION PROJECTS

PROGRAMS

FPR FINANCE
     PERSONNEL

FIV FINANCE
     INVOICES

FIT FINANCE
     INCOME TAX

FCR FINANCE
     CORPORATE RECORDS

FINANCE

CST COMPUTER SOFTWARE
     TESTING

CSM COMPUTER SOFTWARE
     MARKETING

CSD COMPUTER SOFTWARE
     DEVELOPMENT

COMPUTER
SOFTWARE

BEST PRACTICES

Archiving E-mail

The demand for e-mail management is growing. Best practices enable businesses to archive and search e-mail records. Best practices include these processes:

- Capture and archive all incoming, interoffice, and outgoing e-mail messages on an e-mail server.
- Provide access to the e-mail archive via a web client as well as through the e-mail program.
- Track access to the archived e-mail records.
- Provide secure storage for the e-mail archive.
- Retain the archive on multiple storage media, such as optical write once/read many discs and tape.

COMPUTER APPLICATION 5 (SEE APPENDIX A.)
Adding Records, Adding Subject Fields, Sorting by Subjects, and Printing

End-of-Chapter Activity

In this activity, you learn about subject key words. When you are categorizing records by subject or searching for records, you need to choose appropriate subject key words that are the most important terms related to a record.

Read the following e-mail and underline at least three words or phrases that you believe are most descriptive of the content of the message. The key words you select should be those most relevant if you were searching for this message in your e-mail in-box. One term has already been underlined as an example.

Untitled Message

| File | Edit | View | Insert | Format | Tools | Table | Window | Help |

To...	Lindsey Travers
Cc...	
Subject...	UPCOMING DATABASE TRAINING SEMINAR
Attach...	

Greetings:

I wanted to let you know about an upcoming web seminar that you might be interested in attending: "Managing Electronic Records Databases." Because your company is increasingly using document imaging for converting paper records to digital format, you and your staff will need to develop skills in managing the records stored in the document database. This seminar will demonstrate how to prepare records for scanning, how to use the tools and features of your new records management software, how to search for records in the database, and how to generate reports of records that are scheduled for destruction.

The cost of the seminar is covered by your organization's site license and maintenance contract for your new Records Management Trak System Version 2.3. It's easy to register—just go to http://www.rmtraksystem.com and fill out the registration form. You will receive a confirmation e-mail with instructions for logging on to the web seminar. Attendance is at your convenience, as the online seminar is available 24/7. You can start and stop the lessons at any time and return later to continue.

Please contact me if you have any questions.

Best regards,

Megan Herrera
Training Coordinator
Records Management Trak System Software

Chapter 6: Geographic Filing Procedures

Learning Goals
- Learn the U.S. Postal Service's two-letter state abbreviations.
- Follow the six steps involved in processing records for geographic filing.

Introduction

Geographic filing is a flexible method that meets the needs of businesses that organize their records by location rather than by subject or number. For example, a company that has offices in several states may find it convenient to organize records according to state. A catalog-order business that ships merchandise all over the world may require a geographic filing method to keep sales orders and customer records efficiently organized. Real estate companies list their available properties by location, including street address, so their filing method needs to include a geographic arrangement of records.

A company that handles international business will want to subdivide its files into countries and then cities. A company operating exclusively within the United States will have state and then city subdivisions. The names of the geographic locations are filed alphabetically, and the correspondents' names are indexed as subsequent units.

The following examples show the indexing order for geographic filing.

EXAMPLES:					
Correspondent and Location	**Unit 1**	**Unit 2**	**Unit 3**	**Unit 4**	**Unit 5**
Century 21 Autos Augusta, ME*	MAINE	AUGUSTA	CENTURY	21	AUTOS
Pets-R-Us Eastport, ME	MAINE	EASTPORT	PETSRUS		
LaSalle College College Park, MD	MARYLAND	COLLEGE	PARK	LASALLE	COLLEGE
Children's Discovery Center Quincy, MA	MASSACHUSETTS	QUINCY	CHILDRENS	DISCOVERY	CENTER
Hill St. Trattoria Springfield, MA	MASSACHUSETTS	SPRINGFIELD	HILL	STREET	TRATTORIA
International Wireless Springfield, MA	MASSACHUSETTS	SPRINGFIELD	INTERNATIONAL	WIRELESS	
Ms. Carmen Ortiz Worcester, MA	MASSACHUSETTS	WORCESTER	ORTIZ	CARMEN	MS

*The U.S. Postal Service prefers that two-letter state abbreviations be used in addressing correspondence.

Figure 6-1 lists the states and territories with their abbreviations.

Alabama	AL	Montana	MT
Alaska	AK	Nebraska	NE
Arizona	AZ	Nevada	NV
Arkansas	AR	New Hampshire	NH
California	CA	New Jersey	NJ
Colorado	CO	New Mexico	NM
Connecticut	CT	New York	NY
Delaware	DE	North Carolina	NC
District of Columbia	DC	North Dakota	ND
Florida	FL	Ohio	OH
Georgia	GA	Oklahoma	OK
Guam	GU	Oregon	OR
Hawaii	HI	Pennsylvania	PA
Idaho	ID	Puerto Rico	PR
Illinois	IL	Rhode Island	RI
Indiana	IN	South Carolina	SC
Iowa	IA	South Dakota	SD
Kansas	KS	Tennessee	TN
Kentucky	KY	Texas	TX
Louisiana	LA	Utah	UT
Maine	ME	Vermont	VT
Maryland	MD	Virgin Islands	VI
Massachusetts	MA	Virginia	VA
Michigan	MI	Washington	WA
Minnesota	MN	West Virginia	WV
Mississippi	MS	Wisconsin	WI
Missouri	MO	Wyoming	WY

FIGURE 6-1

Two-Letter Postal Abbreviations

Geographic Filing Procedures

Step 1: Inspecting

Check each record to be sure it has been released for filing. Release marks are explained in Chapter 3, pages 34–35.

Step 2: Indexing

Look for the correspondent's location on the piece of correspondence. On incoming business letters, the letterhead usually contains the address. If the incoming letter is personal business, look for the correspondent's location in the return address, which is above the date line. On outgoing correspondence, look for the correspondent's location in the inside address.

WORKPLACE FOCUS

Professional Certification in the Records Management Field

Many records managers are seeking professional certification to enhance their job skills and earning power. The primary certification for records managers is the CRM, Certified Records Manager. To earn the CRM certification, records managers must meet specific educational and work experience requirements and pass an examination. The organization that administers the program for professional certification of records managers is the Institute of Certified Records Managers (ICRM).

Members of the ICRM follow a code of ethics, which is a guide to professional conduct, as follows:[1]

1. **Certified Records Managers have a professional responsibility to conduct themselves so that their good faith and integrity shall not be open to question. They will promote the highest possible records management standards.**

2. **Certified Records Managers shall conform to existing laws and regulations covering the creation, maintenance, and disposition of recorded information, and shall never knowingly be parties to any illegal or improper activities relative thereto.**

3. **Certified Records Managers shall be prudent in the use of information acquired in the course of their duties. They should protect confidential, proprietary and trade secret information obtained from others and use it only for the purposes approved by the party from whom it was obtained or for the benefit of that party, and not for the personal gain of anyone else.**

4. **Certified Records Managers shall not accept gifts or gratuities from clients, business associates, or suppliers as inducements to influence any procurements or decisions they may make.**

5. **Certified Records Managers shall use all reasonable care to obtain factual evidence to support their opinion.**

6. **Certified Records Managers shall strive for continuing proficiency and effectiveness in their profession and shall contribute to further research, development, and education. It is their professional responsibility to encourage those interested in records management and offer assistance whenever possible to those who enter the profession and to those already in the profession.**

[1] Institute of Certified Records Managers, 5 Aug., 2005 http://www.icrm.org/ethics.

In a file containing international correspondents, the name of the country is the first indexing unit. For a U.S. geographic file, such as the one you will work with in Practical Application 6, it is not necessary to code the country name, United States, as the first two indexing units for each piece. *United States* is understood to be indexed as the first two units because all correspondence is to or from U.S. correspondents. Therefore, the name of the state is coded as the first indexing unit, followed by the city name.

After indexing the state and city, index the name of the correspondent as shown in the examples on page 83. Follow the alphabetic indexing rules in Chapter 2.

Step 3: Coding

Code the location of the correspondent by circling the state and writing the number 1 above or below the circle. Circle the city and write the number 2. (Note that ZIP Codes are disregarded.)

Because you have already coded the correspondents' names on the pieces of correspondence you will use in Practical Application 6, you do not need to do any additional coding of names. In an office, however, remember to code correspondents' names as subsequent units following the geographic location.

If the name of a correspondent contains the geographic location, such as Akron Art Museum, it is still indexed and coded as usual. (See the following examples.)

EXAMPLES:

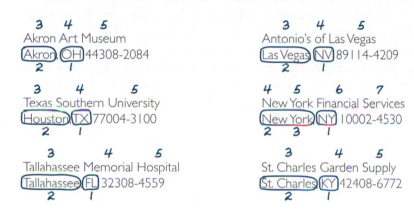

Step 4: Cross-Referencing

If the letterhead shows more than one address for a correspondent, file the original piece of correspondence under the most important address and prepare a cross-reference for the other address. The most important address is usually the main branch, home office, or original location of a business. Code the alternative address by placing wavy circles around the state and city names, coding them 1 and 2, and writing an X in the margin nearby. Prepare cross-references in geographic filing when one of the following situations occurs:

- **The correspondent has more than one location.**
- **The correspondent's name is usually cross-referenced in the alphabetic filing method. (See Chapter 2, pages 16–17 and 28–30, for a review of the types of names that require cross-references.)**

Step 5: Sorting

First, quickly sort the correspondence by state. Then sort the correspondence alphabetically by city within each state.

Step 6: Filing and Retrieval

For each state, the file contains a guide and a general folder, as shown in the illustration at the end of this chapter. Individual folders for cities within that state are placed between the guide and the general folder. The general folder is used for correspondence that does not yet have an individual city folder. Within the general folder, correspondence is filed alphabetically by city name.

In Practical Application 6, you will use 3 general state folders and 10 individual city folders. Correspondence for other cities will be filed in the general folders for their states.

Within the city folders, correspondence is filed alphabetically according to the names of the correspondents. When you have two or more pieces regarding the same correspondent, place the most recent record in front.

When someone wants to borrow a record from the files, follow the charge-out and follow-up procedures presented in Chapter 3. When completing an OUT Sheet in geographic filing, write the geographic location on the *Name of Record* line. Write the name of the correspondent on the first *Address* line and write the street address below. No OUT Sheets are needed in Practical Application 6.

CHECK YOUR UNDERSTANDING

Geographic Filing Procedures   Time Goal: 5 Minutes

Directions: Using the procedures for geographic filing, index and code the following two letterheads. Then fill in the cross-reference sheets. In geographic filing, the first line of the cross-reference sheet always includes the state name (two-letter abbreviation) followed by the city name. Write the correspondent's name and street address on the first two *Address* lines. The SEE notation has the original state and city on the first line and the name and street address on the next two lines.

Answer the following questions for Letterheads 1 and 2.

Questions

1. **For Letterhead 1, which would come first in the file, the letter or the cross-reference sheet?**

   _____

2. **For Letterhead 2, which would come first in the file, the letter or the cross-reference sheet?**

   _____

Letterhead 1

Hotel Meridian

Our original location

560 Shoreline Drive
Honolulu, HI 96813-5660

Our newest location

17701 Sunset Way
Hana, HI 96713-3440

Cross-Reference Sheet
for Letterhead 1

CROSS-REFERENCE SHEET

Name or Subject _____

_____

Address _____

_____

_____

SEE _____

_____

_____

_____

Letterhead 2

Miller and Moradi

Law Offices

80 West 34th Street
New York, NY 10013-1534

Cross-Reference Sheet
for Letterhead 2

CROSS-REFERENCE SHEET

Name or Subject _____

_____

Address _____

_____

_____

SEE _____

_____

_____

_____

See pages 133–134 for the correct answers.

PRACTICAL APPLICATION 6
Geographic Filing

Time Goal: 1 Hour

Supplies   File box
Correspondence pieces 1–45, previously used
3 previously used guides
3 orange guide labels (Envelope 1):
      CALIFORNIA
      COLORADO
      CONNECTICUT
13 previously used folders
13 orange folder labels (Envelope 1):
      CA   BEVERLY HILLS
      CA   DELMAR
      CA   LOSANGELES
      CA   SACRAMENTO
      CA   SANFRANCISCO
      CA   TORRANCE
      CALIFORNIA
      CO   DENVER
      CO   FT COLLINS
      COLORADO
      CT   HARTFORD
      CT   NEW HAVEN
      CONNECTICUT
5 cross-reference sheets (Forms Pad 2)
Checksheet 6 (Checksheet Packet)
Retrieval Exercise 6 (Checksheet Packet)

Directions
Follow step-by-step.

1. **Attach the 3 orange guide labels to the guides and the 13 orange folder labels to the folders.**

2. **Set up the guides and folders as shown in the following illustration.**

3. **For each of correspondence pieces 1–45, follow the geographic filing steps on pages 81–84. Prepare 5 cross-references.**

4. **After you have processed and filed the correspondence, complete Checksheet 6 and give it to your instructor for checking. If you made any mistakes in filing, correct them before beginning Retrieval Exercise 6.**

5. **Complete Retrieval Exercise 6.**

6. **Remove all items from the file box and rearrange the correspondence pieces in numeric order, from 1 to 50. Discard the cross-reference sheets. Store the guides and folders in the appropriate envelopes.**

COMPUTER APPLICATION 6 (SEE APPENDIX A.)
Geographic Sorting

End-of-Chapter Activity

Learn more about professional certification for records managers. Explore the Institute of Certified Records Managers web site at http://www. icrm.org. Read the latest ICRM newsletter for updates on various subjects. Also look at the employment opportunities for records managers who have achieved the CRM designation (CRM Wanted list). Choose one of the job listings. Write a one-paragraph summary of the skills and requirements needed for the position and explain why you would or would not be interested in the position. Share your summary with the class.

Chapter 7: Records Retention, Transfer, and Disposition

Learning Goals
- Learn the components of a records retention schedule.
- Learn the concept of transferring active records to inactive storage.
- Learn the methods of records disposition.

Introduction

All records, whether paper-based, electronic, or microimage, have a life cycle that needs to be systematically managed. After a record has been created, used, stored, and retrieved, the remainder of its life cycle is determined by answers to questions such as the following:

- How long should the record be kept?
- Should the record be transferred to inactive storage?
- Should a paper record be transferred to microfilm, microfiche, magnetic media, or optical disc?
- After a certain time period, should the record be destroyed?

An invaluable tool of the records manager is a schedule of records retention and disposition. With this schedule, a records manager can determine answers to the preceding life cycle questions. A records retention and disposition schedule can save a company money by reducing the costs of keeping records indefinitely in active file storage systems and database archives. Uncluttered files also make storing and retrieving records more efficient. Electronic files are faster to locate and data backup is facilitated when the volume of files is under control.

Storage Vocabulary

Active records—Records used frequently because they provide information needed for the day-to-day operation of a business.

Inactive and semiactive records—Records that are referred to infrequently.

Archives or historical records—Inactive records that are kept permanently because they concern the history of the company.

Vital records—Permanent records that are indispensable to a business's operation, such as legal and financial records.

Working with a Records Retention and Disposition Schedule

Many forms of records retention and disposition schedules exist because records systems, retention requirements, and records cycles vary for each company. A company must also consider federal, state, and local legal requirements when a records retention and disposition schedule is developed.

Using the Records Retention and Disposition Schedule for The Learning Zone as an example (Figure 7-1), let's examine the components of a sample schedule.

1. **Records.** The types of records filed at The Learning Zone are listed on the schedule. These include various accounting records, corporate records, correspondence, and personnel records.

2. **Department Abbreviations.** The department codes tell which department of The Learning Zone created the record.

   COM: Computer Software

   FIN: Finance

   PER: Personnel

   PRO: Programs

   ALL: All departments

3. **Retention Codes.** The retention codes indicate how many months a record is kept in the records center's active files and how many months it is kept in the inactive files. At The Learning Zone, inactive files are stored on the lower shelves of the cabinets in the records center. Vital records and archives that are scheduled to be kept permanently are transferred to special cartons and kept in the storage center downstairs. The storage center is designed to protect the records from fires, floods, dust, insects, mildew, and theft. The following retention codes are used by The Learning Zone:

   A: Active; for example, A—3 means retain in active files for 3 months.

   I: Inactive; for example, I—9 means retain in inactive files for 9 months.

4. **Media Codes.** The Learning Zone uses a variety of media for storing inactive records. The records retention schedule indicates whether the paper record will be stored in its original paper form, reduced in size and stored on microfiche or microfilm, or stored in digital form on magnetic tape. Another type of storage media is optical disc, which stores data on CD or DVD. The following media codes are used by The Learning Zone:

   P: Paper

   F: Microfiche

   M: Microfilm

   MM: Magnetic media

   O: Optical disc

5. **Destruction Codes.** When the retention period for a record expires, to protect the confidentiality of the record's contents, it may be shredded before it is discarded. Less important records may be sent to a local

THE LEARNING ZONE, INC.
RECORDS RETENTION AND DISPOSITION SCHEDULE

Record	Dept.	Retention (Months)	Media	Destruction
ACCOUNTING				
Accounts Payable Invoices	FIN	A—6, 1—6	P	S
Accounts Receivable Records	FIN	A—6, 1—6	F	S
Bank Statements	FIN	A—6, 1—12	P	S
Budget Reports	FIN	A—12, 1—12	P	S
Financial Statements	FIN	Permanent	F	—
Income Tax Returns	FIN	Permanent	P	—
Payroll Records	PER	A—18, 1—18	O	S
CORPORATE RECORDS				
Certificates of Incorporation	FIN	Permanent	P	—
Charter	FIN	Permanent	P	—
Contracts	FIN	A—length of contract, 1—10 years after	P / F	S / S
Minutes of Board of Directors	FIN	Permanent	P/MM	—
CORRESPONDENCE				
Business Letters	ALL	A—3, 1—9	P/MM	R
Business Reports	ALL	A—12, 1—12	P/MM	R
Day-Care Applications	PRO	A—while enrolled, 1—6 after	P / O	R / R
Interoffice Memorandums	ALL	A—3, 1—9	P/MM	S
Seasonal Publications	ALL	A—3	P	T
Software Documentation	COM	A—while current, 1—12 after	MM/O / MM/O	R / R
PERSONNEL RECORDS				
Correspondence	PER	A—3, 1—3	P	R
Disability/Illness Benefits	PER	A—6, 1—6	P	S
Employee Benefit Plans	PER	A—while current, 1—12 after	P / M	S / S
Hires, Promotions, Dismissals	PER	A—while current, 1—12 after action	P / M	S / S
Individual Employee Files	PER	A—while current, 1—6 after	F / F	S / S
Job Applications	PER	A—6, 1—6	F	S
Resumes	PER	A—6, 1—6	F	S

FIGURE 7-1

Records Retention and Disposition Schedule for The Learning Zone, Inc.

recycling center, and some records may be disposed of with the regular trash. The following destruction codes are used by The Learning Zone:

S: Shred

R: Recycle

T: Trash

CHECK YOUR UNDERSTANDING

Records Retention, Transfer, and Disposition   Time Goal: 10 Minutes

Part 1

Directions: Use a term from the chapter to answer each of the following questions.

1. What records are indispensable to a business's operation? _____

2. What records are used frequently in the day-to-day operation of a business? _____

   _____

3. What is the name for historical records that are kept permanently? _____

4. Records may be kept permanently in special cartons, protecting them from dust, fire, floods, mildew, and theft by transferring them where? _____

5. Shred, Recycle, and Trash are examples of what kind of codes? _____

Part 2

Directions: Refer to the Records Retention and Disposition Schedule for The Learning Zone (Figure 7-1) to answer the following questions.

6. How many months are resumes retained in the active files? _____

7. How long are contracts retained in the inactive file after the length of the contract expires? _____

   _____

8. Name one type of record that is to be retained permanently. _____

9. What media is used to store inactive payroll records? _____

10. What destruction method is most often listed at The Learning Zone? _____

See page 134 for the correct answers.

Personal Records Management

Spring is not the only time to clean up paperwork that you have around your house; disorganized personal records are not only messy, but also risky. Identity theft, lost tax deductions, and wasted time searching for records can be the result of poor personal records management.

What personal records should you keep? Here are the five major categories for a home filing system:

- **Financial (tax returns, bank statements, credit card statements, bills, stock and bond records)**

- **Insurance (homeowners, apartment, medical, life, auto)**

- **Legal (wills, power of attorney, medical directives, employment contracts)**
- **Property (lease, mortgage information, deeds)**
- **Vital (birth certificates, marriage license, medical records, military records, educational transcripts, diplomas)**

Folders for each type of record should be organized behind a guide or divider for each category. Each category could be color-coded for efficient refiling.

How long should you keep your personal records? Here are some guidelines to follow.

Keep Forever	Keep Seven Years
Employment records	Accident reports and claims
Educational records	Bank statements
Important correspondence	Tax returns and supporting documents for
Legal records	tax returns
Medical history	
Vital documents	

Most clutter is made up of the receipts, statements, and documents that accumulate from day to day. You should review that paperwork annually, discarding it following these general guidelines:

- **Bills. Keep until payment and balance are verified by the next bill.**
- **Paycheck stubs. Keep until verified by your annual W-2 statement.**
- **Car records. Keep until the car is sold.**
- **Credit card receipts. Keep until verified by credit card statement.**
- **Credit card statements. Keep for a year.**
- **Insurance policies. Keep for the life of the policy plus three years in case of late claims.**
- **Medical bills. Keep in the event of insurance disputes.**
- **Property records/maintenance and improvement records. Keep until property is sold plus seven years if tax-related.**
- **Receipts and warranties for major appliances. Keep for the life of the product or warranty.**
- **Stock and bond records. Keep for six years after the stocks and bonds are sold.**

Everyone needs his or her own system of managing personal records for an efficient, secure, and reliable way to access information when it is needed.

COMPUTER APPLICATION 7 (SEE APPENDIX A.)
Sorting by Date and Deleting Records According to Date

BEST PRACTICES

E-mail Retention Policy

E-mail messages sent and received by an organization's employees are records that need to be managed. The content and purpose of an e-mail determines the retention period. An e-mail retention policy is necessary so employees know what information sent or received via e-mail should be retained and for how long.

Four general classifications of e-mail and their retention periods are as follows:

- Administrative Correspondence (4 years)
- Fiscal Correspondence (4 years)
- General Correspondence (1 year)
- Ephemeral Correspondence (Retain until read, destroy)

Administrative Correspondence includes company policies, legal issues, and messages containing sensitive information.

Fiscal Correspondence is all information related to revenue and expenses for the company.

General Correspondence refers to messages about operational decisions of the company and interaction with customers.

Ephemeral Correspondence includes personal messages, general requests, updates, and recommendations. Most messages fall into this category.

End-of-Chapter Activity

Using the guidelines presented in Chapter 7 for personal records management, go through your personal records at home. In the first column of the form below, list the types of records you are keeping. Then, in the second column, next to each type of record, write the length of time you need to keep the record. Make a copy of the form and refer to it annually to make sure you are following best practices for managing your personal records.

Type of Record	Retention Period

APPENDIX A
Computer Applications

A computer database is a collection of related records, such as the names, addresses, and telephone numbers of a business's customers or the names, departments, and salaries of a company's employees. The computer database stores information about each customer or employee and makes it easy for a user to locate, retrieve, update, add, delete, and change the information, or data. Database management system (DBMS) software programs, such as FileMaker Pro®, Microsoft Access®, Paradox, and QuickBase®, make it possible to link information easily, to make inquiries (for example, Which employees work in the sales department?), and to print reports of part or all of the information.

Although each DBMS has its own set of user instructions, many concepts and terms are basic to understanding electronic databases. Review the following concepts and terms, referring back to their definitions as needed.

Table—A database is a collection of one or more tables. An EMPLOYEE table and a MANAGER table may be contained in a database called ORGANIZATION, for example.

Record—A record is one individual entry or row in a table, such as the name, department, and salary of the employee Carol Ruiz.

Field—A field is an individual item of information in each record, such as the last name, Ruiz.

Key field or primary key—Each record in a table has an identifier, such as Carol Ruiz's Employee number, that is unique to that record and does not appear in any other record.

Directions for the Computer Applications in *Intensive Records Management*, Fifth Edition, are general and need to be adapted to the specific instructions for the database software being used in your classroom.

You will need an external storage medium such as a disk, CD-ROM, thumb drive, or zip disk for storing your databases. Follow your instructor's directions.

COMPUTER APPLICATION 2A

Opening and Defining a Table, Adding Records, and Printing a Report   Time Goal: 1 Hour

Supplies
Cards 1–25 in numeric order, indexed and coded (no cross-reference cards*)
External storage medium (with your name written on it)
Microsoft Access® or other installed DBMS
Printer

Directions
Follow the instructions step-by-step.

Before You Start
Know the basic operating instructions for the DBMS application used in your classroom.

→ You can open the CUSTOMER database that has already been set up on the Data CD, or you can follow the steps to define a database and create a new table. The first five records have already been added to the CUSTOMER table as examples.

Define a Database
Define a new database called CUSTOMER by following these general steps and applying them to your DBMS software:

1. **Start your DBMS program.**
2. **Choose the New Database command and key CUSTOMER as the file-name. Select the location of your file storage so you can create and save the CUSTOMER database.**

Create a New Table
Define the fields in the new table by following these general steps and applying them to your DBMS program:

1. **Key the first field name Customer Number. Select Text as the data type. Key Customer Number (Primary Key) as the field description and choose the Set Primary Key button. The field size is 2. Move to the second row to enter the second field.**
2. **Repeat the procedures in step 1 for each field to create the new table as shown in Figure CA2-1.**
3. **Proofread your keyed table carefully and correct any errors.**
4. **Save the CUSTOMER table to your external storage medium. Close the Table window.**

* For simplification, cross-referencing is not included in this computer application.

Field Name	Data Type	Field Size	Field Description
Customer Number	Text	2	Customer Number (Primary Key)
Indexed Name	Text	90	Name in Indexed Order
Address 1	Text	50	Street Address
Address 2	Text	50	Second Line of Address
City	Text	15	City
State	Text	2	State (two-letter abbreviation)
ZIP Code	Text	10	ZIP Code (nine-digit version)

FIGURE CA2-1
Structure of CUSTOMER Table

→ Follow the next steps to add records to the CUSTOMER table and to preview and print a table. The first five records have already been added to the CUSTOMER table as examples.

Add Records to a Table

1. **Open the CUSTOMER table. You will add records to the CUSTOMER table from cards 1–25. The fields in the table correspond to the data on each card. Read the following field descriptions to understand the procedures for entering the data in each field. Use the Caps Lock key to enter the information for each card in ALL CAPS.**

Customer Number. This field corresponds to the card number on cards 1–25. Add a leading zero (0) to card numbers 01 through 09.

Indexed Name. This field contains the name in indexed order, according to Alphabetic Indexing Rules 1–10 in Chapter 2. Insert a space between each indexed unit.

Address 1. This field contains the street address.

Address 2. This field is for the second line of an address, such as Suite 200 (card 16), The Medical Building (card 19), or Office of the Mayor (card 21).

City. Enter the city name in this field. Be sure to key the name in correct indexed order (for example, Santa Rosa should be keyed as SANTAROSA).

State. Key the two-letter state abbreviation in this field.

ZIP Code. This field is for the 9-digit ZIP Code. The field size is 10 so you can include the hyphen.

2. Using Figure CA2-2 as a guide, fill in all fields for Records 1–25. (**Note:** The first 5 records have already been entered in the CUSTOMER table on the Data CD.) The first 10 records are shown in Figure CA2-2. Special instructions for Records 16, 19, 21, and 22 are as follows:

Record 16:	Address 1	6700 83 PLACE SW
	Address 2	SUITE 200
Record 19:	Address 1	3002 COLORADO BOULEVARD
	Address 2	THE MEDICAL BUILDING
Record 21:	Address 1	200 N SPRING STREET
	Address 2	OFFICE OF THE MAYOR
Record 22:	Address 1	THE FOX PLAZA

3. Save the CUSTOMER table to your external storage medium.

Preview and Print a Table

1. Select the Print Preview command to view the CUSTOMER table before printing.

2. Select two columns to print: Customer Number and Indexed Name. Make sure that all of the characters in the Indexed Name column are visible. Choose the Print command to print the first two columns of the CUSTOMER table. If your DBMS does not allow you to print selected fields, print the entire CUSTOMER table.

3. Give the printed copy of your CUSTOMER table to your instructor for checking.

4. Close the CUSTOMER database and exit the DBMS program.

Records 1–10 of CUSTOMER Table

Customer Number	Indexed Name	Address 1	Address 2	City	State	ZIP Code
01	DENNISON CATHYSUE	4400 W MARKHAM AVENUE		LITTLE ROCK	AR	72201-8243
02	CALIF ATTYS COMMISSION	1630 MONTEREY DRIVE		SANTAROSA	CA	95404-5871
03	COORIER RACHEL DDS MS	41 BURNHAM AVENUE		PROVIDENCE	RI	02910-5876
04	FUNG CHO	27 VISTA DELMONTE		COSTA MESA	CA	92626-7287
05	ENTREPRENEUR USA	650 BROADWAY		ENGLEWOOD	NJ	07631-1677
06	FAST AND EZ TAX SERVICE	556 FOURTH STREET		CHARLOTTE	NC	28228-3001
07	EAST VIEW RECREATION CTR	4029 LAFAYETTE PLACE		PORTLAND	OR	97208-6702
08	EZ SOFTWARE CO	114 TERRACE NW		MIAMI	FL	33168-3756
09	COVRALL CARPETTILE	3699 KENSINGTON AVENUE		PHILADELPHIA	PA	19134-8221
10	COURIER AND SONS INC	1440 REEVES AVENUE		LONG ISLAND	NY	10314-2001

COMPUTER APPLICATION 2B

Adding Records, Sorting Alphabetically, and Printing a Report

Time Goal: 1 Hour

Supplies
Cards 26–50 in numeric order, indexed and coded (no cross-reference cards*)
Data CD containing the CUSTOMER database file
Microsoft Access® or other installed DBMS
Printer

Directions
Follow the instructions step-by-step.

Open a Database and Select a Table
1. Select the Open Database command and choose the location of your external storage medium.
2. Highlight the CUSTOMER database to open it.
3. Open the CUSTOMER table.

Add Records to a Table
1. Select the Last Record button or command to move to Record 25.
2. Choose the Next Record button to move to a new record.
3. Add Records 26–50 to the CUSTOMER table, following the same procedures as in Computer Application 2A. Remember to press the Caps Lock key to enter the field information in ALL CAPS. Refer to these special instructions:

Record 27:	**Address**	13102 32 STREET
	Address 2	HOPE CHAPEL
Record 29:	The two-digit number 99 is the largest numeric key unit to be entered in the Indexed Name field. All other numeric key units should be keyed with leading zeros to allow for an accurate sort. (See the instructions for Records 37 and 38 later in this list.)	
Record 31:	**Address**	140 N CANON DRIVE
	Address 2	SUITE 3000
Record 35:	**Indexed Name**	FAST COPY SHOP NUMBER 2 THE
	Address 1	COOPER BUILDING SUITE 40
Record 37:	**Indexed Name**	01 FULLSERVICE CELLULAR
	Address 1	40 COURTYARD AVENUE
	Address 2	BANKERS BUILDING
Record 38:	**Indexed Name**	03 TO 8 CHILDRENS DANCE ARTS
Record 40:	**Indexed Name**	UNITED STATES GOVERNMENT TREASURY DEPARTMENT OF THE CUSTOMS SERVICE
	Address 1	FEDERAL BUILDING

* For simplification, cross-referencing is not included in this computer application.

Record 41:	**Indexed Name**	ST LOUIS 1 FEDERAL SAVINGS AND LOAN INST
Record 43:	**Address 1**	LINCOLN TOWERS
Record 48:	**Address 1**	STATE CAPITOL
Record 49:	**Address 1**	FEDERAL BUILDING
Record 50:	**Address 1**	CAPITOL BUILDING
	Address 2	ROOM 2990

4. Save the **CUSTOMER** table to your external storage medium.

Sort a Table Alphabetically by Indexed Name

Database software can sort the records in your CUSTOMER table alphabetically according to any fields you select.

1. Select the Indexed Name field.
2. Choose the Sort by Ascending (A-Z) button or command.

Sort a Table Alphabetically by Indexed Name, City, State, Address

According to the filing rules in Chapter 2, names are alphabetized in the following order: indexed name, city, state, street name, and house or building number.

1. Use the Sort feature of your DBMS to sort the fields in the following order. Select the Ascending order sort option for each field.

    1. Indexed Name
    2. City
    3. State
    4. Address 1

2. The table is sorted by the fields you selected. The other fields are omitted from the sort. Notice that the database software arranged Records 06 and 33 (FAST AND EZ TAX SERVICE) by house number (556 before 7552) instead of by street name (Fifth should have come before Fourth). In Computer Application 3A, you will design a table with a separate numeric field for house numbers and a separate text field for street names. Then you can instruct the software to sort street names *before* house numbers to follow the alphabetic indexing rules in Chapter 2.

Print the Results of Sorting a Table

1. Select the first two columns of the sorted **CUSTOMER** table, Customer Number and Indexed Name.
2. Choose the Print command to print a copy of the sorted table. If your DBMS does not allow you to print selected fields, print the entire **CUSTOMER** table.
3. Give the printed copy of the sort to your instructor for checking.
4. Close the **CUSTOMER** database and exit the DBMS program.

COMPUTER APPLICATION 3A

Opening and Defining a Table, Adding Records, and Printing a Report

Time Goal: 1 Hour

Supplies

Correspondence pieces 1–15 in numeric order, indexed and coded
External storage medium
Microsoft Access® or other installed DBMS
Printer

Directions

Follow the instructions step-by-step.

→ You can open the CLIENTS database that has already been set up on the Data CD, or you can follow the steps to define a database and create a new table. The first five records have already been added to the CLIENTS table as examples.

Define a Database

1. **Start your DBMS program. Insert your external storage medium.**
2. **Choose the New database command and key CLIENTS as the filename. Select the location of your file storage to create and save the CLIENTS database.**

Create a New Table

Define the fields in the new table by following these general steps and applying them to your DBMS program:

1. **Key the first field name as Client Number. Select Text as the data type. Key Client Number (Primary Key) as the field description and choose the Set Primary Key button. The field size is 3. Move to the second row to enter the second field.**
2. **Repeat the procedures in step 1 for each field to create the new table as shown in Figure CA3-1. Note that the Address 2 field is a numeric field. It will contain the house or building number. This numeric field enables the software to sort the house or building numbers into numeric order when identical street names are in the Address 1 field.**

FIGURE CA3-1
Structure of CLIENTS Table

Field Name	Data Type	Field Size	Field Description
Client Number	Text	3	Client Number (Primary Key)
Indexed Name	Text	90	Name in Indexed Order
Address 1	Text	50	Street Name
Address 2	Number	5 or "Integer"	House or Building Number
City	Text	25	City
State	Text	2	State (two-letter abbreviation)
ZIP Code	Text	10	ZIP Code (nine-digit version)
Date	Text	10	Date of Record

Note that the Date field contains the date of each record. It is keyed as YYYY(Year)/MM(Month)/DD(Day); for example, June 4, 2006, would be entered 2006/06/04. The year 2006 has been entered as an example (see Figure CA3-2, page 105); however, you should use the current year.

3. Proofread your keyed table carefully and correct any errors.

4. Save the CLIENTS table to your external storage medium. Close the Table window.

Add Records to a Table

1. Open the CLIENTS table. You will add records to the CLIENTS table from correspondence pieces 1–15. (Note: The first five records have already been added to the CLIENTS table on the Data CD as examples.) Read the following field descriptions to understand the procedures for entering the data in each field. Use the Caps Lock key to enter the information for each record in ALL CAPS.

Client Number. This field corresponds to the piece number on correspondence pieces 1–15. Add a leading zero (0) to numbers 01 through 09. Add X to cross-reference records.

Indexed Name. This field contains the name in indexed order, according to Alphabetic Indexing Rules 1–10 in Chapter 2 and the rules for coding incoming and outgoing correspondence in Chapter 3. Because the largest numeric key unit is 901, key all other numeric key units with leading zeros. For example, for piece 5, key **001 PACIFIC NATIONWIDE BANK.**

Address 1. This field contains the street name only. Omit building names and suite numbers.

Address 2. This field contains the house or building number and is set up as a numeric field so the software will sort according to the rules for identical names. Street names will sort before house or building numbers.

City. The city name is keyed in indexing order so the city names will sort correctly in Computer Application 6 (for example, LOSANGELES, MARINA DELREY, NEW HAVEN).

State. Key the two-letter state abbreviation in this field.

ZIP Code. This field is for the nine-digit ZIP Code, including the hyphen.

Date. This field is for the date of the correspondence. Enter dates YYYY(Year)/MM(Month)/DD(Day); for example, June 4, 2006, would be entered 2006/06/04. All correspondence takes place in the current year. Add leading zeros to months or days 01 through 09. Because correspondents' records are filed with the most recent record in front, the date field will be sorted in descending order (from highest to lowest).

2. Using Figure CA3-2 as a guide, fill in all fields for correspondence pieces 1–15. The first 10 records are shown in Figure CA3-2. Note that Record 9 shows the Indexed Name in original order: CALDANO AND DELACRUZ ATTORNEYS AT LAW. Database Record 10 shows the same address and date information, but the Client Number is keyed as 09X and the Indexed Name is the cross-referenced order: DELACRUZ AND CALDANO ATTORNEYS AT LAW. You will have 16 database records in the CLIENTS table (the 15 correspondence pieces plus 1 cross-reference).

3. Save the CLIENTS table to your external storage medium.

Print Selected Fields from a Table

1. Print the CLIENTS table showing Records 1–16:

   a. If your DBMS program allows you to select fields for printing, select the following fields to print:

      Client Number

      Indexed Name

      Date

   b. If your DBMS program requires that you run a query to select those three fields, create a new query by selecting Query, New from the Database window. Select the fields Client Number, Indexed Name, and Date to include in the query. Name the query **Computer Application 3A**. Run and print the results of the query.

2. Give the printed copy of your CLIENTS table to your instructor for checking.

3. Close the CLIENTS database and exit the DBMS program.

FIGURE CA3-2

Records 1–10 of CLIENTS
Table

Client Number	Indexed Name	Address 1	Address 2	City	State	ZIP Code	Date
01	FIVESTAR TOURS AND TRAVEL	WASHINGTON BOULEVARD	5880	DENVER	CO	80202-3444	2006/05/11
02	ESTES MARIA PHD	MAY STREET	3552	LOSANGELES	CA	90066-2550	2006/05/30
03	DARTT UNIVERSITY	UNIVERSITY CIRCLE	12	NEW HAVEN	CT	06501-2334	2006/06/05
04	ESTES M DR	TIMBERLINE DRIVE	9980	BOULDER	CO	80302-5223	2006/06/08
05	001 PACIFIC NATIONWIDE BANK	WILSHIRE BOULEVARD	8500	BEVERLY HILLS	CA	90202-6600	2006/06/15
06	ESTES MARIA PHD	MAY STREET	3552	LOSANGELES	CA	90066-2550	2006/06/15
07	DELMAR CREATIVE GRAPHICS	MELROSE AVENUE	9330	DELMAR	CA	92014-1650	2006/06/18
08	DARTT UNIVERSITY	UNIVERSITY CIRCLE	12	NEW HAVEN	CT	06501-2334	2006/06/25
09	CALDANO AND DELACRUZ ATTORNEYSATLAW	CENTINELA AVENUE	3508	TORRANCE	CA	90034-5115	2006/06/28
09X	DELACRUZ AND CALDANO ATTORNEYSATLAW	CENTINELA AVENUE	3508	TORRANCE	CA	90034-5115	2006/06/28

105

COMPUTER APPLICATION 3B

Adding and Finding Records, Sorting Alphabetically, and Printing a Report

Time Goal: 1 Hour

Supplies

Correspondence pieces 16–30 in numeric order, indexed and coded
Data CD containing the CLIENTS database file
Microsoft Access® or other installed DBMS
Printer

Directions

Follow the instructions step-by-step.

Add Records to a Table

1. Open the CLIENTS database and select the CLIENTS table.
2. Select the Last Record button or command to move to Record 16. (Piece 15 is Record 16 because of cross-reference piece 09X.)
3. Choose the Next Record button to move to a new record.
4. Add correspondence pieces 16–30 to the CLIENTS table, following the same procedures as in Computer Application 3A. Remember to press the Caps Lock key to enter the field information in ALL CAPS. Refer to these special instructions:

Piece 17:	**Address 1**	BURNSIDE DRIVE
	Address 2	544
	ZIP Code	Use Sacramento ZIP Code 94267-0031 for Jas. Cisneros.
Piece 18:	**Address 1**	88 AVENUE
	Address 2	1033
Piece 19:	**Address 1**	SOUTHWEST REGIONAL OFFICE
	Address 2	
Piece 23:	**Address I**	11 STREET
	Address 2	409
Piece 24:	**Indexed Name**	044 AVENUE COMMUNITY CHURCH
	Address 1	WEST 44 AVENUE
	Address 2	8966
Piece 28:	**Date**	2006/09/01
Piece 30:	**Indexed Name**	TURNER TYLER

    Prepare a cross-reference record Client Number 30X with Indexed Name STFRANCIS DEANA MARIE.

5. Save the CLIENTS table to your external storage medium before continuing.

Display a Table in Form View

DBMS programs can display each record one at a time as a form. Use the Form View or AutoForm button or command in your DBMS program to display the CLIENT table in Form View. AutoForm automatically creates a form based on the data in the table. Use Form View to complete the next section.

Find Records in a Table, Using the Navigation Buttons

1. Click on the Navigation buttons at the bottom of the form to find the following requested records. (See Figure CA3-3.)

    a. Click on First Record in Table to see the first record in your CLIENTS database, Client Number 01, FIVESTAR TOURS AND TRAVEL.

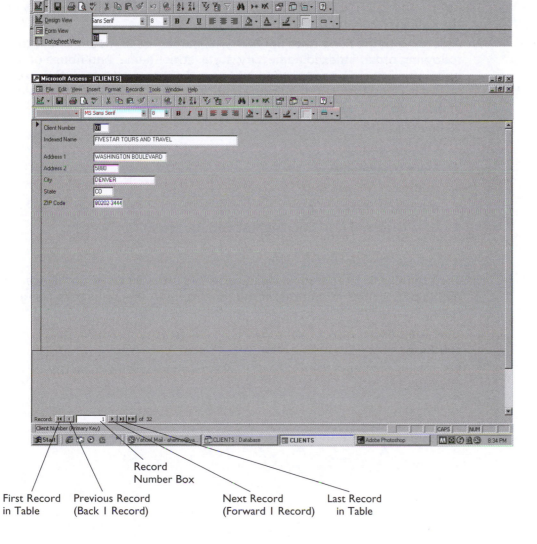

FIGURE CA3-3

Navigation Buttons in Form View

    b. Click on **Next Record** to see the next record in sequence, Client Number 02, **ESTES MARIA PHD**. Click on **Next Record** again to see the next record in sequence, Client Number 03, **DARTT UNIVERSITY**.

    c. Click on **Previous Record** to see the previous record in sequence, Client Number 02, **ESTES MARIA PHD**. Click on **Previous Record** again to see the previous record, Client Number 01, **FIVESTAR TOURS AND TRAVEL**.

    d. Click on **Last Record in Table** to see the last record in your CLIENTS table, Client Number 30X, **STFRANCIS DEANA MARIE**.

    e. Click on the **Record Number Box** to find a specific record number. Delete the number showing in the number box. Key **22** and press Enter to see Client Number 21, **RADIO STATION KGGI**. Key another record number of your choice and press Enter to view another form.

2. Practice using the **Navigation** buttons to move through the CLIENT forms. You will perform more complex record searches in Application 3C.

Sort a Table Alphabetically According to Filing Rules

1. Return the CLIENTS table to Datasheet View to list the entire contents of the CLIENTS table on the screen.

2. According to the filing rules in Chapter 2, names are alphabetized in the following order: indexed name, city, state, street name, and house or building number. If a correspondent has more than one record, the most recent is listed first. Use the Sort feature of your DBMS to sort the fields in the following order:

    1. Indexed Name (Ascending)

    2. City (Ascending)

    3. State (Ascending)

    4. Address 1 (Ascending)

    5. Address 2 (Ascending)

    6. Date (Descending—from highest or most recent to lowest)

Print the Results of Sorting a Table

1. Print the CLIENTS table showing Records 1–32 (the 30 correspondence pieces plus 2 cross-references) sorted according to the alphabetic filing rules.

2. Give the printed copy of your CLIENTS table to your instructor for checking.

3. Do not save changes. Close the CLIENTS database and exit the DBMS program.

Searching for Data

Time Goal: 30 Minutes

Supplies
Data CD containing the CLIENTS database file
Microsoft Access® or other installed DBMS

Directions
Follow the instructions step-by-step.

Database software lets you find any record in your database by searching on any field or combination of fields. You can search for any phrase, word, or part of a word, called a text string.

1. Open the CLIENTS database and select the CLIENTS table.

2. You can display the CLIENTS table in either Datasheet or Form View.

3. Click the Find button on the toolbar or choose Find from a command menu. The DBMS displays the Find What dialog box.

4. In the Find What dialog box, key the text you want to find. Practice the following ways of searching for data:

   a. **Key the Text You Want to Find.** Select the Indexed Name field. Choose the Find command. Key the text you want to find in the Find What dialog box.

      Practice: 1. Key RADIO STATION KGGI in the Find What dialog box.

      2. Choose Match Whole Field.

      3. Choose Match Case.

      4. Select Find Next.

      The database software will find Client Number 21, RADIO STATION KGGI. Choose Close.

   b. **Key Part of the Text You Want to Find.** Select the Indexed Name field. Choose the Find command. Key one word of the record you want to find in the Find What dialog box.

      Practice: 1. Key **GRAPHICS** in the Find What dialog box.

      2. Choose Any Part of Field.

      3. Choose Match Case.

      4. Choose Find Next 3 Times.

      The database software will find the following records that have GRAPHICS as part of the Indexed Name field: Records 07, 12, and 14, DELMAR CREATIVE GRAPHICS. Choose Close.

   c. **Key One Letter of the Record You Want to Find.** If you are unsure of the spelling of a name, key the first letter. Choose the Find command. Key one letter of the name you want to find in the Find What dialog box.

      Practice: 1. Key **S** in the Find What dialog box.

      2. Choose Start of Field.

      3. Choose Match Case.

      4. Choose Search in All Fields.

      5. Choose Find Next until no more records are found.

The records for STFRANCES and STFRANCIS will be found. Choose Close.

d. **Use Wildcard Characters.** Wildcard characters are symbols such as * ? # [ ] !. Wildcard searches find records that have certain characters or that match a certain pattern. You usually use this type of search when you are uncertain of a spelling or when you want to make your search more general. For example, if you key R*Z, all names that begin with *R* and end with *Z*, such as Ramirez, will be found. Or you can find cross-referenced records by searching the Client Number field for the character *X*. Choose the Find command. In the Find What dialog box, key the wildcard symbol * (asterisk) followed by **X.**

Practice: 1. Key ***X** in the Find What dialog box.

2. Choose **Any Part of Field.**

3. Choose **Match Case.**

4. Choose **Search in All Fields.**

5. Choose **Find Next.**

The records 09X and 30X will be found. Choose Close.

You will perform multiple field searches, or queries, in Computer Application 4B.

COMPUTER APPLICATION 3C EXERCISES

Directions: Search for the records requested in the following three exercises. On the answer form provided, record the client numbers for the records that the database software finds. When you finish, close the CLIENTS table and exit the DBMS program.

1. **City Name Search:** Find any records for clients in the city of **LOSANGELES.**

2. **Partial Text Search:** Find any records for clients who are **ATTORNEYS.**

3. **Wildcard Search:** Find any records dated in May of the current year **(2006/05/?).**

COMPUTER APPLICATION 3C ANSWER FORM

Directions: List the client number of each record found in Exercises 1, 2, and 3.

Exercise 1	Exercise 2	Exercise 3
Client Number	Client Number	Client Number
_____	_____	_____
_____	_____	_____
_____	_____	_____
_____	_____	_____

COMPUTER APPLICATION 3D

Modifying Records, Deleting Records, Sorting, and Printing

Time Goal: 30 Minutes

Supplies
Data CD containing the CUSTOMER database file
Microsoft Access® or other installed DBMS
Printer

Directions
Follow the instructions step-by-step.

Find Records to Be Modified

1. Open the CUSTOMER database and select the CUSTOMER table. You will make changes to the contents of five records in your CUSTOMER database. Those changes are shown in Figure CA3-4, following the exercise.

2. Use the Find feature to find each of the five records to be modified. You can select the Customer Number field or do a Search in All Fields. Another option is to key only the first few characters of each customer name and use the Any Part of Field search.

   a. See Figure CA3-4 and modify the first record as follows: Find the record for Customer Number 01, Cathy-Sue Dennison. You can work either in Datasheet View or in Form View. Click on the Address 1 field and move the insertion point to the *W*. Press Delete to remove the *W* and the space from the address. Press Enter to accept the change. Use Find to start a new search.

   b. Continue making the changes to the other four records shown in Figure CA3-4.

Find Records to Be Deleted

1. Figure CA3-4 also shows two records that are to be deleted from the CUSTOMER database.

2. Find each record in Datasheet View and select the record. Press the Delete key to delete the record. Choose the OK button to accept the deletion.

Sort and Print a Table

1. Sort the CUSTOMER table by selecting the Customer Number field. Use Ascending order.

2. Print the first two columns of the CUSTOMER table, Customer Number and Indexed Name.

3. Give the printed copy to your instructor for checking.

4. Save the CUSTOMER table to your external storage medium.

5. Close the CUSTOMER database and exit the DBMS program.

FIGURE CA3-4

Modifications to CUSTOMER Database

Modifications

Change From:

Customer Number 01
Cathy-Sue Dennison
4400 W. Markham Avenue
Little Rock, AR 72201-8243

Customer Number 05
Entrepreneur U.S.A.
650 Broadway
Englewood, NJ 07631-1677

Customer Number 08
E Z Software Co.
114 Terrace, NW
Miami, FL 33163-3756

Customer Number 13
Fresh Fish & Chips!
90 Clairmont Boulevard
Decatur, GA 30030-2464

Customer Number 20
Mr. Edw. Courvallis
232 Sykes Road
Jackson, MS 39212-3727

Change To:

Customer Number 01
Cathy-Sue Dennison
4400 Markham Avenue
Little Rock, AR 72201-8243

Customer Number 05
Entrepreneur U.S.A.
650 Broadway **Street**
Englewood, NJ 07631-1677

Customer Number 08
E Z Software Co.
114 Terrace, NW
Miami, FL 3316**6**-3756

Customer Number 13
Fresh Fish & Chips!
90 **Claremont** Boulevard
Decatur, GA 30030-2464

Customer Number 20
Mr. Edw. Courvallis
2320 Sykes Road
Jackson, MS 3921**4**-3727

Deletions

Customer Number 32
TV Station WRCW

Customer Number 42
Sun-Time Bar-B-Q Ribs

COMPUTER APPLICATION 4A

Adding Records, Adding a Field, Numeric Sorting, and Printing

Time Goal: $1\frac{1}{2}$ Hours

Supplies
Correspondence pieces 1–40 in numeric order, indexed and coded for consecutive numeric filing
Data CD containing the CLIENTS database file
Microsoft Access® or other installed DBMS
Printer

Directions
Follow the instructions step-by-step.

Add Records to a Table

1. **Open the CLIENTS database and select the CLIENTS table.**

2. **Select the Last Record button or command to move to Record 32.**

3. **Choose the Next Record button to move to a new record.**

4. **Add correspondence pieces 31–40 to the CLIENTS table, following the same procedures as in previous Computer Applications. Remember to press the Caps Lock key to enter the field information in ALL CAPS. Refer to these special instructions:**

   Piece 31:   **Indexed Name**   001 PACIFIC NATIONWIDE BANK

   Piece 32:   Use the original location:

   Address 1   C Street

   Address 2   34

   City   Remember that SAN FRANCISCO is keyed as one unit.

   Piece 35:   **Address 1**   SW 11 Street

   Piece 36:   Omit Suite 320 from the Address fields.

   Prepare a cross-reference record, 36X, CALIFORNIA CONSERVATION COALITION.

   Piece 37:   **Indexed Name**   RAMIREZ SOCORRO A MISS

   Piece 38:   **Address 1**   CITY HALL ROOM 2112

   Address 2

   Piece 40:   **Address 1**   WESTERN REGIONAL OFFICE

5. **After you enter piece 40, you should have 43 records in the CLIENTS table.**

Add a New Field

You have already coded correspondence pieces 1–40 for consecutive numeric filing. Each correspondence piece shows either a number or a *G* in the upper right corner. Now you will add a new field that contains this numeric information. The new field, File Number, will follow the Date field.

1. **To add a new field, choose the Design button from the toolbar or from the CLIENTS Database window.**
2. **Move to the next blank row (under the Date row) in the Field Name column. Key File Number as the field name. Press the TAB key. Select the Text data type. Choose the Field Size box and change the number to 4. Key the Description: File Number (Numeric or General Alphabetic = G).**

Field Name	Data Type	Field Size	Field Description
File Number	Text	4	File Number (Numeric or General Alphabetic = G)

3. **Choose the Save command from the File menu.**
4. **Choose the Datasheet View.**

Add Numeric Data

If your CLIENTS table is in alphabetic order by Indexed Name, select the Client Number field and sort the table by Client Number in ascending order. This will make it easier to add information to the new File Number field.

Tab across to the File Number field. After you enter the File Number for a record, press the Down Arrow key to move down to the next record and stay in the File Number field. Key the numeric file number **G** or key **GX** for Records 1–43. Refer to the following special instructions for the cross-reference records:

> *Record 10:* **Piece 09X, DELACRUZ AND CALDANO ATTORNEYSATLAW**
> **File Number 650X**
>
> *Record 19:* **Piece 18, STFRANCIS DEANA MARIE**
> **File Number 659 (This piece is filed with her son's records under TURNER TYLER.)**
>
> *Record 32:* **Piece 30X, STFRANCIS DEANA MARIE**
> **File Number 659X**
>
> *Record 39:* **Piece 36X, CALIFORNIA CONSERVATION COALITION**
> **File Number GX**

Sort a Table by File Number

Sort the fields in the following order:

1. **File Number (Ascending)**
2. **Indexed Name (Ascending)**
3. **Date (Descending)**

For File Numbers that are the same, the most recent record for a client will be listed first. The general records are listed in alphabetic order by indexed name with the exception of piece 36X, which has a File Number of GX.

Print the Results of Sorting a Table

1. Print the CLIENTS table showing Records 1–43 in File Number order by selecting the following fields:
   - File Number (Ascending)
   - Client Number (Unsorted)
   - Indexed Name (Ascending)
   - Date (Descending)

2. Give the printed copy of your CLIENTS table to your instructor for checking.

3. Save the CLIENTS database.

4. Close the CLIENTS database and exit the DBMS program.

COMPUTER APPLICATION 4B

Creating a Query, Running a Query, and Printing the Results of a Query

Time Goal: 30 Minutes

Supplies
Data CD containing the CLIENTS database file
Microsoft Access® or other installed DBMS
Printer

Directions
Follow the instructions step-by-step.

A query is a question about the records in a database; for example, "How many clients live in Los Angeles?" or "Is there a health spa in Denver?" To find the answers to such questions, you need to create a query of the database. The results of the query will display in a list format called a dataset.

Create a New Query

1. **Open the CLIENTS database and have the Database window on the screen.**
2. **Choose the Query button or command for the CLIENTS database.**
3. **Choose the New Query button.**
4. **Add the CLIENTS table to the query and close the Add Table window.**
5. **A list of the fields in the CLIENTS table is displayed. A QBE (Query-by-Example) grid is also displayed. The QBE grid contains the fields you select, the sorting arrangement, and any other criteria for selecting records.**

Query 1: Show the File Number, Indexed Name, and State for All Clients

1. **Point to the File Number field and double-click to place the File Number field in the QBE grid.**
2. **Point to the Indexed Name field and double-click to place the Indexed Name field in the second column of the QBE grid. Click in the Sort row under the Indexed Name field to choose Ascending.**
3. **Point to the State field and double-click to place the State field in the third column of the QBE grid.**
4. **To run query 1, click the Run button. The DBMS displays the results shown in Figure CA4-1 at the end of this application.**
5. **To close query 1, point to the Control Menu box for the Select Query window and double-click. Choose No to exit the query without saving query 1.**

Query 2: Find All Clients in Denver

1. **Start a New Query for the CLIENTS table.**
2. **Place the Indexed Name (Ascending) and City fields in the QBE grid. Point to the Criteria row under City and key DENVER for the City field criteria.**
3. **Run the query.**

4. **The resulting dataset is shown in Figure CA4-2 at the end of this application.**

5. **To close query 2, point to the Control Menu box for the Select Query window and double-click. Choose No to exit the query without saving query 2.**

Query 3: Find File Numbers and Names of Clients in California

1. **Create and run a new query to find the file numbers and names of clients (alphabetic order) who live in California.**

2. **Print the resulting dataset and give it to your instructor for checking.**

3. **Close the Query window and exit without saving query 3.**

4. **Close the CLIENTS database and exit the DBMS program.**

FIGURE CA4-1

Results of Query 1
File Number, Indexed Name in Ascending Order, and State for All Clients

File Number	Indexed Name	State
655	001 PACIFIC NATIONWIDE BANK	CA
655	001 PACIFIC NATIONWIDE BANK	CA
G	044 AVENUE COMMUNITY CHURCH	CA
656	901 COMPUTER SOFTWARE SERVICE	CO
656	901 COMPUTER SOFTWARE SERVICE	CO
650	CALDANO AND DELACRUZ ATTORNEYSATLAW	CA
650	CALDANO AND DELACRUZ ATTORNEYSATLAW	CA
650	CALDANO AND DELACRUZ ATTORNEYSATLAW	CA
GX	CALIFORNIA CONSERVATION COALITION	CA
G	CALIFORNIA STATE OF PARKS AND RECREATION DEPARTMENT WILL ROGERS STATE HISTORIC PARK	CA
G	CCC	CA
G	CISNEROS JAS	CA
651	DARTT UNIVERSITY	CT
651	DARTT UNIVERSITY	CT
651	DARTT UNIVERSITY	CT
650X	DELACRUZ AND CALDANO ATTORNEYS AT LAW	CA
652	DELMAR CREATIVE GRAPHICS	CA
652	DELMAR CREATIVE GRAPHICS	CA
652	DELMAR CREATIVE GRAPHICS	CA
G	DUPREES OFFICE DEPOT	CA
G	ESTES M DR	CO
653	ESTES MARIA PHD	CA
653	ESTES MARIA PHD	CA
654	FIVESTAR TOURS AND TRAVEL	CO
654	FIVESTAR TOURS AND TRAVEL	CO
654	FIVESTAR TOURS AND TRAVEL	CO
G	FRIENDLY FITNESS CLUB THE	CA
G	FUTURE WORLD MAGAZINE	CO
G	R J DEVILLE MFG	CA
G	RADIO STATION KGGI	CT
657	RAMIREZ SOCORRO A MISS	CT
657	RAMIREZ SOCORRO A MISS	CT
G	STFRANCES DEANA MARIE	CO
659X	STFRANCIS DEANA MARIE	CO
659	STFRANCIS DEANA MARIE	CO
G	STFRANCIS HEALTH SPA	CA
G	TEMPLE CITY COMMUNITY DEVELOPMENT AGENCY	CA
658	TTI MEDIA COMMUNICATIONS	CA
658	TTI MEDIA COMMUNICATIONS	CA
659	TURNER TYLER	CO
G	UNITED STATES GOVERNMENT INTERIOR DEPARTMENT OF THE FISH AND WILDLIFE SERVICE	CA
G	UNITED STATES GOVERNMENT TREASURY DEPARTMENT OF THE INTERNAL REVENUE SERVICE	CO
G	UNITED STOCKS AND INVESTMENTS INC	CT

Indexed Name	City
FIVESTAR TOURS AND TRAVEL	DENVER
FIVESTAR TOURS AND TRAVEL	DENVER
FIVESTAR TOURS AND TRAVEL	DENVER
STFRANCES DEANA MARIE	DENVER
STFRANCIS DEANA MARIE	DENVER
STFRANCIS DEANA MARIE	DENVER
TURNER TYLER	DENVER

FIGURE CA4-2
Results of Query 2
Clients in Denver

Adding Records, Adding Subject Fields, Sorting by Subjects, and Printing

Time Goal: 1 Hour

Supplies

Correspondence pieces 26–50 in numeric order, indexed and coded for subject filing
Data CD containing the CLIENTS database file
Microsoft Access® or other installed DBMS
Printer

Directions

Follow the instructions step-by-step.

Add Records to a Table

1. **Open the CLIENTS database and select the CLIENTS table.**
2. **Select the Last Record button or command to move to Record 43.**
3. **Choose the Next Record button to move to a new record.**
4. **Add correspondence pieces 41–50 to the CLIENTS table. They will become Records 44 to 53. The File Number field for those records will be blank. Refer to these special instructions:**

Piece 42:	**Indexed Name**	021 CENTURY DEVELOPMENT CORP
	Address 1	PO BOX 35
Piece 43:	**Address 1**	11 STREET
	Address 2	409
Piece 46:	This is an interoffice memo. Leave the Address fields blank. Enter only the Client Number, Indexed Name, and Date.	
Piece 47:	**Address 1**	ROUTE 2 BOX 352C
Piece 48:	This is another interoffice memo. Process as you did with piece 46.	

5. **After you enter piece 50, the CLIENTS table should have 53 records.**

Add Subject Fields

You have already coded correspondence pieces 26–50 for subject filing. Each correspondence piece has a subject selected from the alphabetic subject index in Chapter 5. That subject is written in the upper right corner or coded in the body. Correspondence pieces 35 and 45 also have cross-referenced subjects. Now you will add two new fields, Subject l and Subject 2, to your CLIENT database.

1. **To add a new field, choose the Design button from the toolbar or from the CLIENTS Database window.**

2. **Move to the next blank row (under the File Number row) in the Field Name column and enter the information for the two new fields as shown here:**

Field Name	Data Type	Field Size	Field Description
Subject 1	Text	3	Original Subject
Subject 2	Text	3	Cross-Referenced Subject

3. **Choose the Save command from the File menu.**
4. **Choose the Datasheet View.**

Add Subject Information

If your CLIENTS table is in alphabetic order by Indexed Name, select the Client Number field and sort the table by Client Number in ascending order. This will make it easier to add information to the new subject fields.

Scroll down to Client Number 26, CALIFORNIA STATE OF PARKS AND RECREATION DEPARTMENT WILL ROGERS STATE HISTORIC PARK. You will add subject information to Records 27–53 for correspondence pieces 26–50. Tab across to the subject 1 field. Enter the subject code, **PLA.** After you enter the subject code for a record, press the Down Arrow key to move down to the next record and stay in the Subject 1 field. For all subjects, use the three-letter subject codes from Practical Application 5. (**Note:** Leave the subject fields blank for 30X and 36X [cross-references of indexed names].) The only two records that will have information in the Subject 2 field are those that have cross-referenced subjects, piece 35 (Record 37) and piece 45 (Record 48).

Sort a Table by Subject

Sort the fields for Client Numbers 26–50 in the following order:

1. **Subject 1 (Ascending)**
2. **Indexed Name (Ascending)**
3. **Date (Descending)**

Print the Results of Sorting a Table

1. **Print the CLIENTS table showing Records 27–53 in Subject order by selecting the following fields:**
   - **Client Number (Unsorted) Criteria of >25 (This means you are selecting Client Numbers 26–50.)**
   - **Subject 1 (Ascending)**
   - **Indexed Name (Ascending)**
   - **Date (Descending)**
2. **Give the printed copy of your CLIENTS table to your instructor for checking.**
3. **Save the CLIENTS database.**
4. **Close the CLIENTS database and exit the DBMS program.**

COMPUTER APPLICATION 6

Geographic Sorting

Time Goal: 30 Minutes

Supplies
Data CD containing the CLIENTS database file
Microsoft Access® or other installed DBMS
Printer

Directions
Follow the instructions step-by-step.

Sort a Table by State

1. Open the CLIENTS database and select the CLIENTS table.
2. Sort the fields in the CLIENTS table in the following order:
   1. State (Ascending)*
   2. City (Ascending)
   3. Indexed Name (Ascending)
   4. Date (Descending)
3. View the results of the sort on the screen or print a copy if your instructor prefers. Include the Client Number on the printout.

Sort a Table by City

1. Sort the fields in the following order:
   1. City (Ascending)
   2. Indexed Name (Ascending)
   3. Date (Descending)
2. View the results of the sort on the screen or print a copy if your instructor prefers. Include the Client Number on the printout.

Sort a Table by ZIP Code

1. Sort the fields in the following order:
   1. ZIP Code (Ascending)
   2. Indexed Name (Ascending)
   3. Date (Descending)
2. View the results of the sort on the screen or print a copy if your instructor prefers. Include the Client Number on the printout.
3. Close the CLIENTS database and exit the DBMS program.

* Sorting by the two-letter postal abbreviations will result in proper alphabetic sequence with the database states: CA (California), CO (Colorado), CT (Connecticut), and OR (Oregon). However, be aware that not all two-letter postal abbreviations will sort into proper alphabetic order, such as AK (Alaska) and AL (Alabama). In the future, if you plan to sort a U.S. database by state, enter the spelled-out state names for each record.

COMPUTER APPLICATION 7

Sorting by Date and Deleting Records
According to Date

Time Goal: 20 Minutes

Supplies
Data CD containing the CLIENTS database file
Microsoft Access® or other installed DBMS

Directions
Follow the instructions step-by-step.

Sort a Table by Date

1. Open the CLIENTS database and select the CLIENTS table.

2. Assume that it is January of next year. You want to delete records from the CLIENTS database that are more than six months old, that is, records that are dated prior to July 1 of the current year. Sort the dates of the CLIENTS records in ascending order.

Delete Inactive Records

1. Scroll through the first 20 records in the CLIENTS table. Those records have the earliest dates. Look for records that have dates prior to July 1.
       Another option is to perform a query to locate records that are dated prior to July 1 (for example, < 2006/07/01).

2. Select the records that have been identified as having dates prior to July 1. Use the Delete Record command or the Delete key to delete those inactive records.

3. Close the CLIENTS database and exit the DBMS program.

APPENDIX B

Supplemental Computer Applications

1. Geographic Sorting by State, City, and ZIP Code

Time Goal: 15 Minutes

Sort the CUSTOMER database by state, city, and ZIP Code. Sort the fields in the following order:

1. **State (Ascending)**
2. **City (Ascending)**
3. **ZIP Code (Ascending)**

Print the results of the sort.

2. Querying a Database

Time Goal: 30 Minutes

Use the query feature of your DBMS to search for records in the CUSTOMER database that answer the following questions. Create the appropriate queries for the CUSTOMER database and run them. Print the results of the queries.

a. **Do any customers have a key unit beginning with the letter C? (C*)**
b. **Are any customers located in Seattle?**
c. **What is the address for Ramon's?**

3. Opening and Defining a File and Adding Records

Time Goal: 1 Hour

Create a new database file named CONTACTS that contains the names, addresses, and telephone numbers of 10 friends and/or relatives.

4. Querying a Database

Time Goal: 15 Minutes

Use the query feature of your DBMS to search for records in the CONTACTS database that answer at least two questions of your choice. Suggested queries are listed here:

a. **What is the telephone number of _____?**
b. **What contacts' last names begin with the letter S?**
c. **Are any contacts' located in _____? (Choose a city name.)**

Chapter 1, Basic Records Management Concepts, page 5

1. B
2. D
3. C
4. G
5. I
6. F
7. A
8. E
9. H
10. J

Chapter 2, Rules 1 and 2, page 11

Name	Indexing Order of Units			
	Key Unit	Unit 2	Unit 3	Unit 4
(5) L. Carmen Quinares	QUINARES	L	CARMEN	
(6) Lydia Quinares	QUINARES	LYDIA		
(4) L. C. Quinares	QUINARES	L	C	
(8) Quinn Fine Flooring	QUINN	FINE	FLOORING	
(3) Quinares & Benes Investments	QUINARES	AND	BENES	INVESTMENTS
(7) L. Carmen Quinaro	QUINARO	L	CARMEN	
(2) # Off Weight Loss	POUNDS	OFF	WEIGHT	LOSS
(1) Off & On Electricians	OFF	AND	ON	ELECTRICIANS
(9) Sunday News (Tucson)	SUNDAY	NEWS	TUCSON	
(10) Sunday News (Tyler)	SUNDAY	NEWS	TYLER	

Chapter 2, Rules 3 and 4, page 14

Correct Coding	If You Made a Mistake, Reread:
(6) Patricia E<u>verett-Haynes</u> 2	Rule 3, page 12
(7) <u>Mama's</u> Home-Style Pies 2 3	Rule 3, page 12
(9) R. G. <u>Samuels</u> 2 3	Rule 4A, page 12
(1) <u>A</u> B C Inc. 2 3 4	Rule 4B, pages 13
(4) <u>D.R.</u> Home Security 2 3	Rule 4B, pages 13
(2) <u>A-Plus</u> Learning Ctr. 2 3	Rules 3 and 4B, pages 12 and 13
(10) <u>Toy-a-rama</u>	Rule 3, page 12
(5) <u>Ed's</u> Tile Distr. 2 3	Rules 3 and 4B, pages 12 and 13
(8) <u>Radio</u> Station KRCW 2 3	Rule 4B, pages 13–14
(3) <u>A-Z</u> Office Supplies	Rules 3 and 4B, pages 12 and 13

Chapter 2, Cross-Referencing, page 19

Original—Correct Coding	Cross-Reference
<u>EPCOT</u> (Experimental Prototype City of Tomorrow)	EXPERIMENTAL PROTOTYPE CITY OF TOMORROW SEE: EPCOT
2 Mehdi <u>Tazbaz</u>	MEHDI TAZBAZ SEE: TAZBAZ MEHDI
3 2 Mrs. Juan <u>Bustamonte</u> (Mrs. Cecilia Bustamonte)	BUSTAMONTE CECILIA MRS SEE: BUSTAMONTE JUAN MRS
3 2 Dr. Shoshana <u>Taylor-Frye</u>	FRYE SHOSHANA TAYLOR DR SEE: TAYLORFRYE SHOSHANA DR
U.P.S. (United Parcel Service)	UNITED PARCEL SERVCE SEE: UPS

Chapter 2, Rules 6 and 7, pages 22–23

Name	Indexing Order of Units				
	Key Unit	Unit 2	Unit 3	Unit 4	Unit 5
(7) T. Shannon Fitz Simmons	FITZSIMMONS	T	SHANNON		
(4) Nasim El Hassanzadeh	ELHASSANZADEH	NASIM			
(1) 9 O'Clock Maids	9	OCLOCK	MAIDS		
(6) Ever-Brite Carpet Cleaners No. 9	EVERBRITE	CARPET	CLEANERS	NO	9
(8) San Francisco Deluxe Seafood	SANFRANCISCO	DELUXE	SEAFOOD		
(10) St. Nick's Toys 4 Tots	STNICKS	TOYS	4	TOTS	
(3) 21st Century Airlines	21	CENTURY	AIRLINES		
(2) 9–12 Day Care Serv.	9	DAY	CARE	SERV	
(9) Santa Barbara Botanical Gardens	SANTABARBARA	BOTANICAL	GARDENS		
(5) Los Feliz Telecom Corp.	LOSFELIZ	TELECOM	CORP		

Chapter 2, Rules 8, 9, and 10, page 27

Part 1

1. **ba**
2. **ab**
3. **ab**
4. **ba**
5. **ab**

Part 2 Correct Coding

```
            2    3    4    5      6
```
(2) <u>Martin</u> Luther King, Jr., High School
```
            2    3
```
(6) <u>Sylvan</u> City Motel
```
            2    3    4    5      6
```
(5) <u>Society</u> of Marriage & Family Counselors
```
              2       3
```
(10) <u>University</u> of Pennsylvania
```
                              5    6    2      3    4
```
(8) U.S. (<u>United States Government</u>) Office of Management and Budget
```
                                2       3    4    5      6
```
(9) U.S. (<u>United States Government</u>) National Aeronautics & Space Administration
```
        6      7      8      4      5        2    3
```
(3) Foreign Exchange Office, Treasury Department, Kingdom of <u>Norway</u>
```
              4      5    2      3
```
(4) <u>Pensacola</u> Department of Public Housing
```
          2      3    4      5
```
(1) <u>1st</u> Federal Savings & Investments
```
            2       3
```
(7) <u>United</u> Financial Services

Chapter 2, Cross-Referencing Business Names, pages 30–31

Original—Correct Coding	Cross-Reference
2 3 4 <u>Manwani</u> and Mazin Architects	MAZIN AND MANWANI ARCHITECTS SEE: MANWANI AND MAZIN ARCHITECTS
2 3 <u>Aquarius</u> Scuba Equipment (Subsidiary of Sports Gear Inc.)	SPORTS GEAR INC SEE: AQUARIUS SCUBA EQUIPMENT
<u>Viejas</u> (Viejas Family Fun Center)	VIEJAS FAMILY FUN CENTER SEE: VIEJAS
2 <u>Vantage-Crystal</u> Wireless	CRYSTALVANTAGE WIRELESS SEE: VANTAGECRYSTAL WIRELESS
<u>PacTel</u> (PacificTelephone Co.)	PACIFIC TELEPHONE CO SEE: PACTEL

Chapter 3, Rules 1–4 for Incoming Correspondence, page 36

       2   3
1. **<u>LTP</u> of America**

                                   2
2. **The name in the signature line, Mike <u>Yamamoto</u>**

Chapter 3, Filing Microfiche Alphabetically, page 45

(6)   SHANE – SOBEL
(10) UPLAND – VALDEZ
(3)   ROMERO – ROSE
(1)   QUINLAN – REYES
(4)   ROSS – RYKER
(2)   RIVAS – ROLLINS
(9)   TRANH – UNGER
(7)   STAFFORD – SZABO
(8)   TESDADA – TORRES
(5)   SABBAS – SEVILLA

Chapter 3, Color-Coding Alphabetic Files, page 52

Name	Colors on File Folder Label	
(3) Michael F. <u>DiCapprio</u> 2 3	RED	BLUE
(8) <u>San Diego</u> State University 2 3	ORANGE	RED
(6) Mr. Simon <u>O'Shane</u> 3 2	GREEN	ORANGE
(1) Trina <u>Bullette</u> 2	RED	PURPLE
(5) <u>Mountain-View</u> School 2	GREEN	GREEN
(4) <u>John</u> Wayne Sr. High School 2 3 4 5	BLUE	GREEN
(9) <u>Silver</u> Springs YMCA 2 3	ORANGE	BLUE
(2) <u>Children's</u> Book Club 2 3	RED	BLUE
(7) Hassana S. <u>Rama</u>, M.D. 2 3 4	ORANGE	RED
(10) Ms. Val <u>Westley</u> 3 2	PURPLE	RED

Chapter 4, Filing Printouts in Numeric Binders, pages 60–61

CHAPTER
4

Account No.	Binder No.
1. 3107	02
2. 6506	05
3. 0008	01
4. 1101	01
5. 7999	05
6. 4844	04
7. 3691	03
8. 4695	03
9. 2748	02
10. 5263	04

Chapter 4, Terminal-Digit Numeric Filing, page 63

36-37-48	(9)
92-09-27	(5)
23-16-30	(6)
72-35-19	(2)
54-07-49	(10)
50-47-02	(1)
29-16-30	(7)
56-10-48	(8)
59-23-26	(3)
66-07-27	(4)

Chapter 4, Color-Coding Consecutive Numeric Files, page 65

File Number	Colors on File Folder Label	
(9) 68130	LIGHT GREEN	YELLOW
(4) 20739	PINK	RED
(5) 24295	PINK	PURPLE
(6) 31968	LIGHT BLUE	ORANGE
(8) 57291	BROWN	DARK BLUE
(2) 07313	RED	DARK BLUE
(7) 43411	PURPLE	LIGHT BLUE
(10) 86105	YELLOW	LIGHT GREEN
(1) 01630	RED	ORANGE
(3) 19055	ORANGE	DARK GREEN

Chapter 4, Color-Coding Terminal-Digit Numeric Files, page 66

File No.	Colors on File Folder Label	
(8) 534-40-94	DARK GREEN	PURPLE
(2) 407-66-26	PINK	LIGHT GREEN
(6) 021-17-79	DARK BLUE	DARK GREEN
(5) 180-59-51	BROWN	ORANGE
(1) 357-62-23	PINK	LIGHT BLUE
(9) 292-62-94	DARK GREEN	PURPLE
(7) 375-18-79	DARK BLUE	DARK GREEN
(4) 219-34-50	BROWN	RED
(3) 935-38-44	PURPLE	PURPLE
(10) 599-62-94	DARK GREEN	PURPLE

CHAPTER 5

Chapter 5, Subject Filing Procedures, pages 72–75

Questions about Correspondence Piece A

1. Yes. It is a copy of an outgoing letter.
2. APPLICATIONS—RECORDS MANAGER
3. SHI REBECCA MS
4. Wrote *ARM* in the upper right corner, underlined *Shi*, numbered *Rebecca* 2, and numbered *Ms*. 3.
5. Alphabetic according to the name of the correspondent, SHI REBECCA MS
6. No.

Questions about Correspondence Piece B

1. Yes. Initials appear on the letter.
2. ADVERTISING—INTERNET
3. AI ADVERTISING AGENCY
4. Wrote AIN in the upper right corner. Drew a wavy line under the cross-referenced subject, *sales campaigns,* and wrote *MSC* and an *X* in the right margin. Underlined *A-I,* numbered *ADVERTISING* 2, and numbered *AGENCY* 3.

5. **Alphabetic according to the name of the correspondent,
   A1 ADVERTISING AGENCY**

6. **Yes. Marketing—Sales Campaigns.**

Chapter 5, Arranging CD-ROMs in Subject Order, page 75

(3)   BOOKS—SPEED SPANISH

(7)   MUSIC—TCHAIKOVSKY - NUTCRACKER

(4)   GAMES—BASEBALL PRO

(10) SOFTWARE—PHOTO FIXER

(8)   MUSIC—TCHAIKOVSKY - SWAN LAKE

(5)   GAMES—WORD CHALLENGE

(1)   BOOKS—MANAGEMENT MADE EASY

(2)   BOOKS—MONEY MANAGEMENT

(9)   SOFTWARE—GRAPHICS DESIGNER

(6)   MUSIC—BEETHOVEN PIANO CONCERTOS

Chapter 6, Geographic Filing Procedures, pages 84–85

Questions

1. **The cross-reference sheet is first because** *Hana* **comes before** *Honolulu.*

2. **The letter is first because** *Miller* **comes before** *Moradi.*

Letterhead 1 and Cross-Reference Sheet

Hotel Meridian

Our original location	**Our newest location**
560 Shoreline Drive	17701 Sunset Way
Honolulu, HI 96813-5660	Hana, HI 96713-3440

CROSS-REFERENCE SHEET

Name or Subject   HI Hana

Address   Hotel Meridian
17701 Sunset Way

SEE   HI Honolulu
Hotel Meridian
560 Shoreline Drive

Letterhead 2 and Cross-
Reference Sheet

Miller and Moradi

Law Offices

80 West 34th Street
New York, NY 10013-1534

CROSS-REFERENCE SHEET

Name or Subject __NY New York_____

_____

Address __Moradi and Miller_____

_____80 West 34 Street_____

_____

SEE ___NY New York_____

_____Miller and Moradi_____

_____80 West 34 Street_____

_____

CHAPTER
7

Chapter 7, Records Retention, Transfer, and Disposition, page 92

Part 1

1. vital records
2. active records
3. archives
4. storage center
5. destruction codes

Part 2

6. 6 months
7. 10 years
8. Answers will vary but should include one of the following: Financial Statements, Income Tax Returns, Certificates of Incorporation, Charter, or Minutes of Board of Directors.
9. optical disc
10. shred